FLYFISHING

FLYFISHING

BRIAN FURZER

Consultant
Brian Harris

Kingfisher Books

Reminder
Throughout this book, methods of
fishing are discussed which,
although acceptable on some waters,
are not allowed on others. Before you
begin fishing, it is advisable always
to check your permit for conditions
of issue to ensure that you do not
contravene regulations.

First published in hardcover in 1980.
This edition published in 1986 by Kingfisher Books Limited
Elsley Court, 20-22 Great Titchfield Street, London W1P 7AD
A Grisewood & Dempsey Company

© Grisewood & Dempsey Limited 1980

BRITISH LIBRARY CATALOGUING IN PUBLICATION DATA
Furzer, Brian
  Flyfishing. – 2nd ed. – (A Kingfisher guide)
  1. Fly fishing
  I. Title
  799.1'2   SH456
  ISBN 0-86272-187-3

Edited by Norman Barrett

Printed and bound in Italy by
Vallardi Industrie Grafiche S.p.A. Milan

CONTENTS

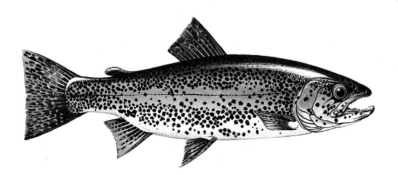

Introduction

Anyone looking for a relaxing pastime that requires little mental or physical effort will not find it in flyfishing. To the uninitiated, fishing might seem a lazy way of spending a day on the river. There is the common picture of the angler snoozing on the bank, with his float bobbing gently on the surface of the water, and coming to life only when there is a tug on the line which is perhaps attached to his big toe. Whether this might vaguely portray aspects of other kinds of angling, it certainly bears no resemblance at all to flyfishing.

Flyfishing is much more than just a pastime or hobby. It is at the same time a sport, a science, and an art. It is completely absorbing and demands concentration of both mind and body. It differs from other kinds of fishing in that the angler has to operate his tackle to present the quarry with an artificial offering (the fly) that is quite inedible and sometimes does not even resemble anything that the fish is likely to feed on. At other times the fly is used to tempt a fish that is not interested in food anyway.

Other differences are that flyfishing tends to be cleaner, because there is no bait to handle, and flyfishers are more mobile, because they usually have less tackle to carry.

The Scientific Approach

Flyfishing often demands a scientific approach because of the many variable factors that have to be taken into account, such as what the fish are feeding on, where and at what depth they will be feeding and, if an exact imitation is not producing results, what colour may irritate them into taking the fly.

Most artificial flies are made of materials such as hair and feathers, but occasionally live insects may be used, such as mayflies or craneflies, in a technique called 'dapping'.

The most popular flyfishing quarries are trout and salmon. Another game fish prized for its sporting ability and eating qualities is the sea trout. But it is not only the freshwater game fish that are sought on fly tackle. Many kinds of coarse fish and salt-water fish are caught on fly, and some of the more exotic species are as highly prized as any game fish.

The special tackle used in flyfishing

Left: A solitary flyfisher casts his artificial fly to the wily fish of an English river.

Right: The results of patience and endurance are fish such as this superb brown trout.

allows the casting of a lightweight fly with pinpoint accuracy and sometimes over great distances. It consists basically of a weighted fly-line and a rod with a flexible, whip-like action.

A fish hooked on flyfishing tackle will generally give a better account of itself than one hooked on heavier gear, and this of course heightens the enjoyment of the sport. The playing of the fish, which may shake itself free at any time during the fight, can be as exhilarating and exciting as the actual taking of the fly by the fish. As a result, flyfishing tends to demand absolute concentration from the angler. And with the constant casting and retrieving, a full session can be extremely taxing.

The pleasures found in flyfishing may be increased in other ways. The sport may be transported from the waterside into your own home, where you can tie the flies that you will use to catch the fish. Fly-tying is a real art when done well.

Flyfishing has its own terminology, and you will find a Glossary at the back of the book (pages 120–123) which explains terms peculiar to flyfishing, and many others besides. There is also a list of recommended books (page 124) on various specific aspects of flyfishing should you require more specialized knowledge.

Development of Flyfishing

There is evidence that flyfishing was practised over two thousand years ago by the Macedonians, and later by the American Indians, probably with bone hooks dressed with animal skin and hair.

But flyfishing first started to become popular as a gentleman's sport in 18th-century England. Long rods of greenheart and other woods were

Flyfishing is practised in all conditions. and over all types of terrain. As the sun sets (below) the fish may start to feed heavily. A salmon angler enters the territory of the fish in an Irish river (top right). A well protected angler surveys the snow covered bank in hilly country (centre). A boat weathers out a storm (centre right). Fishing a Scottish river (bottom right).

used in conjunction with lines made from single or multiple horsehair tied direct to the rod tip. The rod in this instance was largely a shock absorber, and the line was not often cast but swung over to the desired fishing position for the fly. Later, very small reels were developed to store more line, and then the horsehair was tapered by having more strands in the middle than at the end. As a result, casting became normal practice.

Silk oil-dressed lines were introduced in the mid-1800s, and casting

Flyfishing is not the prerogative of the vigorous male. Left: An old hand punches out his line. Above: A lady angler plays a fighting salmon.

proper as we now know it, began to develop. The distances cast, however, did not approach those possible today, mainly because of the weight of the rods.

Rods were improved with the introduction of split cane and ferrules for piecing it together. But the invention of the sinking line was perhaps an accident. Silk lines that had not been treated to float, as they should have been, sank, and it was found that trout could be caught on a sinking line (and with larger flies).

There were further improvements in rods, with newer and lighter materials than split-cane – first glass fibre and then carbon fibre. All three materials are still widely in use.

With the introduction of these new rod materials and of the sinking line, fishing methods were also revolu-

tionized, and many more fly patterns have evolved as a result.

Thus the modern flyfisher is faced with several decisions – choice of quarry, choice of method, choice of tackle, and choice of fly. Having decided on the first three, you will find that it is a very rare occurrence that you will have exactly the right answer to the day's fishing in your fly box, and you will experience many frustrations. If you are fortunate to come across the perfect answer, it will be for only one day; so savour it and enjoy and share it with your friends if possible, while it lasts.

The enjoyment of your flyfishing will be enhanced if you learn to read the water and the conditions and to take pleasure in your surroundings. But once you catch your first fish, you will be hooked for life.

The Fish

Of the many species of fish caught with artificial flies, the game fish – principally salmon and several kinds of trout – are the most popular. But flyfishing is not confined just to game fish, and nor is it practised only in freshwater. A wide range of coarse fish are caught on fly, and in salt-water, fish from mackerel to small sharks are taken.

Salmon

Of the game fish, the most highly prized is the salmon, although because of its high market value flyfishing for salmon can be expensive. The most sought-after species is the Atlantic salmon, widespread throughout Europe and on the eastern coast of North America. Other species of salmon flyfished for include the Chinook, coho, and sockeye of North America (all Pacific salmon) and the rare but powerful huchen of eastern Europe.

Trout

There are two main species of trout, the rainbow and the brown. But there are countless local varieties, fish that have become conditioned by environment – the water they live in and the quality of the food they eat. The rainbow originated in North America, and was introduced into European and New Zealand waters in the late 1800s. The species thrived, except in Britain where fish farms and fisheries breed them to compensate for the scarcity of self-maintaining populations. Rainbow trout tend to be non-migratory in Britain and live in rivers or land-locked waters. But the steelhead, a subspecies of North America, runs to sea, and is regarded as one of the hardest fighting fish capable of being caught on a fly.

The brown trout is widely distributed, having been transported, mainly from British stock, to many countries. In its river form it is a

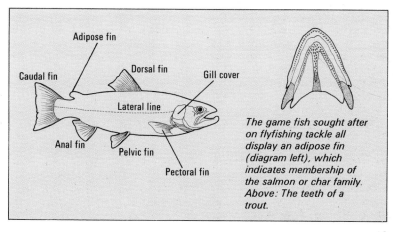

Adipose fin

Dorsal fin

Caudal fin

Gill cover

Lateral line

Anal fin

Pelvic fin

Pectoral fin

The game fish sought after on flyfishing tackle all display an adipose fin (diagram left), which indicates membership of the salmon or char family. Above: The teeth of a trout.

Habitat

Salmon *(Salmo salar)*

The Atlantic salmon is found in the rivers on the western coast of Europe and on the east coast of North America. It migrates to the sea, where it matures until it is ready to return to spawn. The huchen inhabits the cooler rivers of the USSR and the Danube system.

Brown trout *(Salmo trutta)*

Found worldwide—in Europe, Asia, North and South America, Australia and New Zealand. Adapts to a wide variety of waters. In a large lake or reservoir, it may grow very large and is sometimes called a 'lake trout'. Brown trout that have learned to migrate to the sea are called 'sea trout'.

Sea trout *(Salmo trutta)*

Found naturally in northern and western Europe, it is regarded as a most exciting quarry because of its tendency to take a fly best after dark and extremely hard-fighting capabilities. It travels in rivers usually in wild terrain.

Rainbow trout *(Salmo gairdneri)*

Found worldwide, although not necessarily naturally. Can be force-fed to grow rapidly, and is popular for stocking waters for fly-fishing. It adapts to all waters, and is generally more ready to feed throughout the day than the brown trout.

Brook trout *(Salvelinus fontinalis)*

Found naturally in North America, it has now been introduced into Europe where it is thriving and growing in still waters. Popular because it is ready to feed throughout the day, it will take a variety of flies at all depths and is active in most weather conditions.

Grayling *(Thymallus thymallus)*

Virtually the same as for trout in the Northern Hemisphere, as far north as the Arctic regions. In not very heavily populated waters, it reaches larger weights, however, and is in general a hard-fighting fish when not breeding.

Features	Weight
During its fascinating life-cycle, the Atlantic salmon takes on varying appearances. As a parr it is often confused with a small trout, and as a smolt resembles a herring. When returning upriver, the salmon has an overall silver sheen with blue-black spots.	A good specimen of Atlantic salmon weighs 20lb (9kg) or more, a very good specimen upwards of 40lb (18kg), although they do achieve weights well in excess of these. Huchen are commonly caught at around 25lb (11kg), but probably grow to over 100lb (45kg).
The natural form of the wild brown trout has a golden colour, darker on the back, paler on the belly, with dark spots surrounded by paler rings, some spots being red. But coloration and spotting vary considerably according to location.	In its river form, it may maintain a size of only $\frac{1}{2}$lb (225g) in barren regions. A good mountain stream brown trout will reach over 2lb (0.9kg), an exceptional specimen in a large river over 12lb (5.4kg), and lake trout well over this, although they are commonly caught at 10–20lb (4.5–9kg).
Being the sea-run version of the brown trout, it has similar markings, but tends to be completely silver with a dark back. It is torpedo-shaped.	Varies considerably, but commonly caught at around 4lb (1.8kg). A good fish will reach weights in excess of 10lb (4.5kg).
Ordinarily, it has a pale green back, with silver flanks and pale belly and pink tinges along lateral line and gill covers. But it can be much brighter, with only a hint of pink along lateral line, or it can be darker with an almost black back and vivid red markings along lateral line.	When newly stocked, weighs upwards of $\frac{3}{4}$lb (340g), but many waters now introduce stock fish of around 12lb (5.4kg). A good rainbow grown on from very young in its habitat weighs 5lb (2.3kg), and 4 times as much in the larger waters of the Americas and New Zealand.
Coloured a uniform green with a pale belly, and striped more than spotted with a faint paler green. Has a more pointed jaw than the rainbow, and the eyes are set slightly more on top of the head.	The European-bred version has so far reached weights of about 5lb (2.3kg), but is well in excess of that in its native North America. The more usually stocked weights are similar to those of the rainbow.
Easily recognizable by its extra-ordinarily large dorsal fin. When not breeding, it is a large-scaled silver fish, which, when alive, exhibits an attractive bluish hue. During breeding, it turns very dark and is not so becoming. The fins are brownish-red.	In most waters averages probably only $\frac{1}{2}$lb (225g), a good specimen weighing 2lb (900g). In more northerly regions of Europe, it reaches much greater weights and is sometimes caught at around 5lb (2.3kg).

small, voracious fish, which in barren regions is so numerous that it cannot attain a very large size. It has a much longer lifespan than the rainbow and is slower growing. This increases the expense of artificially rearing it, and so it is not quite so commonly stocked in waters flyfished for trout. It will adapt to a wide variety of waters, and if it lives in a large lake or reservoir it may grow to a very large size. And in waters connected to the sea, especially acid waters, there are often sea trout. These are sea-run brown trout that have, over the years, migrated to the sea for its rich feeding.

The rainbow and brown trout belong to the same genus as the salmon (*Salmo*). Other trout of this genus are popular in North America, including the cutthroat trout and the golden trout.

Other Game Fish

The distinguishing feature that is immediately noticeable on the game fish is the addition of a small, fleshy fin on the back between the dorsal and tail fins known as the *adipose fin*.

As well as appearing on all game fish of the salmon and trout species, it is also present on two other species not universally regarded as game fish, the char and the grayling.

Several popular North American trout are really members of the char family (genus *Salvelinus*). These include the brook trout, the Dolly Varden (the native trout of the Pacific coastal waters), and the lake trout of the large northern lakes. The brook trout grows rapidly and is a hard fighting fish. It has been introduced throughout Europe, and despite its name thrives particularly well in still waters.

In Britain, which is generally regarded as the birthplace of flyfishing, the grayling was for some considerable time regarded as a pest because it competed with the trout for food. As a result, grayling were exterminated wherever they appeared in trout waters. Fortunately, there are still some British waters that harbour populations of grayling, and many anglers now prefer them to trout, particularly in the colder months when trout are not rising.

A catch of salmon and sea trout from the river Spey. Both fish can be found in the river at the same time, having returned from the sea to spawn. The salmon is usually the larger fish, as in the photograph, but notice that it has fewer spots than the sea trout and the spots do not extend below the lateral line. The fish are slightly discoloured owing to the passage of time after capture.

Brown and rainbow trout show distinct differences when compared. The brown trout (above) displays spots to its gills, and there are usually no spots on the tail, whereas the rainbow has no spots on its gills and has a spotted tail. Notice that this particular rainbow has a deformed gill due to a complaint contracted in the stock ponds at an early age. It is perfectly healthy.

Salt-Water Fish

Salt-water fish provide great sport for the flyfisher, growing to weights far in excess of freshwater fish. They range from the smaller sharks and the billfish down to the mackerel. In the tropical waters of Florida and the Caribbean, the shy bonefish has become a particularly popular quarry. They are difficult to tempt in the clear waters, and then they are liable to take the line at such a speed that the reel may not be able to cope. Landing a bonefish of 10lb (4.5kg) is regarded by many anglers as the ultimate flyfishing experience.

Coarse Fish

In some countries where game fish are not present, flyfishers have no choice but to seek coarse fish willing to take a fly. And there are some anglers who prefer seeking coarse fish with a fly. Flyfishing tackle is generally regarded as being more sporting than coarse tackle, and it requires more skill.

The coarse fish most frequently sought on fly are pike (called northern pike in North America), dace, chub, rudd, zander, perch, and, in North America, bass.

The pike, which tends to lie near the bottom of a lake or river, is a favourite with flyfishers. It will react to a large, bright lure, and a good-sized specimen would probably weigh in excess of 20lb (9kg). The perch, which is more active than the pike, does not grow to nearly such large sizes, and a 4lb (1.8kg) specimen is regarded as exceptional in most waters. The zander is a voracious feeder and grows to fairly large proportions, up to 45lb (20kg), in its native Dutch waters.

Game Fish Classification

The following are some of the more important game fish caught on a fly. All are members of the Salmonidae family, except the grayling.

Atlantic salmon *Salmo salar*
Brown trout *Salmo trutta*
Sea trout *Salmo trutta*
Rainbow trout *Salmo gairdneri*
Cutthroat trout *Salmo clarki*
Brook trout *Salvelinus fontinalis*
Dolly Varden *Salvelinus malma*
Grayling *Thymallus thymallus*

The Tackle

The basic tackle of a flyfisherman comprises rod, reel, line, leader, and hooks plus, of course, a selection of artificial flies and lures. Because the sport often involves the gentle and accurate placement of these light-weight flies, it is necessary to use a specially made, tapered line coupled with a specifically designed light-weight rod.

Each rod is designed to accept a line of a particular weight, known as its *rating*. This is governed by the fact that the rod is flexed by the weight of line that is in the air while casting.

Rods

Rods vary greatly worldwide. They are usually made in two or three sections, which can be taken apart for storage. Preference for any particular

Opposite page: Flyfishing does not necessarily require a large amount of complicated equipment—a rod made up with a floating line and one for a sinking line if necessary, together with a bag large enough for all tackle, food and drink, and a landing net. On the tackle bag is a priest-cum-marrow-spoon. A priest is an essential item, and is used to kill the fish immediately upon capture. A marrow spoon is used to discover what the fish are feeding on.

material or action is largely a personal matter, while length depends more on the type of fishing and the conditions. Casting action varies from person to person. Those with a hurried casting action are suited to a rod with a fast, or 'tip', action; those with a less hurried action to a rod with a slower, or 'through', action (see the diagrams below). The reason for this is that the time lapse between the back-cast and forward cast is greater if the rod is flexing throughout its length than if flexing just half its length.

The number of guide rings and

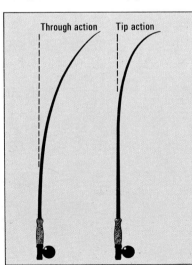

Through action   Tip action

Rod Action

When referring to a rod's 'action', *tip action* means that the tip of the rod is worked to about halfway through its length, the other half doing comparatively little. *Through action* means that the rod is working all through its length.

The action of the rod is determined by a deliberate manufacturing process, and once you decide which type of rod you prefer, it is usually possible to choose one that will suit your casting action. A rod with a 'fast taper'—meaning that it is thick at the butt, requiring a fast taper to the tip—will be more of a tip action rod than one with a slow taper (not so thick at the butt), which will provide a through action.

The three types of rod available: a carbon fibre (or graphite) rod (left), a split-cane rod (centre), and a glass-fibre rod (right). All three rods are approximately 10 feet (3.05m) long and equipped with floating lines of different colours.

their position on the rod also have an effect on its action. Having too many or too heavy rings tends to make the rod floppy, and placing the rings nearer to the tip gives it more tip action.

There are, of course, actions in between the two extremes, and most flyfishermen will find the one that suits them ideally.

There are three materials used almost exclusively in the manufacture of rods: split cane, glass fibre, and carbon fibre (also called graphite).

Split-Cane Rods

Split-cane rods are not in such great demand nowadays, because of their cost and because modern materials are lighter. Each rod is hand-made from sections of selected cane, and a lengthy process results in a rod made up usually of six triangular strips of cane glued together.

The attraction of split cane is that it is a traditional material, and some firms will undertake to design and build a rod for an individual fisherman.

Split cane has been used for many years for flyfishing rivers and streams where distance casting is not required. The main drawback is that it can be fairly heavy as a rod material, although a short one can be particularly delicate. It also requires much more maintenance than synthetic rods, and is more fragile.

Glass-Fibre Rods

Glass fibre provides the happy medium for flyfishermen. While less expensive than rods of the other materials, they can provide all the versatility.

Glass fibre was introduced because

The importance of having a sound rod and tackle is shown here as the rod bends 180° while landing a fish.

it is lighter, stronger, and easier and cheaper to produce. It is an ideal material for newcomers to flyfishing, because it is the most forgiving for an inexpert caster. And on big still waters its lighter weight is less tiring during a day of long casting.

Carbon-Fibre Rods

More recently, carbon fibre has come to the fore as a rod material. Many claims are made as to the outstanding qualities of carbon-fibre rods, but it is a fact that the better rods are lighter and easier to cast with. An expensive carbon-fibre rod costs about the same as a good split-cane rod, but around three times as much as an expensive glass-fibre rod. As with the other materials, it can be tailored to provide any type of action.

Some of the better carbon-fibre rods seem to have a latent power built-in. As a result, the caster needs to use less force to cast similar distances than with other rods.

Rod Length and Weight

The length of rod is dictated not by the flyfisherman, but by conditions and the type of water to be fished.

For salmon fishing, rods of 14ft (4.3m) are common, while lake and reservoir rods are usually about 9–10ft (2.7–3m), and brook rods can be as short as 6ft (1.8m).

The long salmon rods, of course, are heaviest, and some weigh over 1lb (450g), while the shortest brook rods weigh perhaps less than 2oz (57g). An average lake or reservoir rod weighs around 6oz (170g), although carbon-fibre rods may weigh the same as a small split-cane brook rod.

The longer salmon rods used for large rivers are fished two-handed, and their length allows far easier manipulation of the line. To use such a rod for a full day while attempting to reach maximum distances on lakes or reservoirs would be impossibly tiring, so shorter and lighter single-

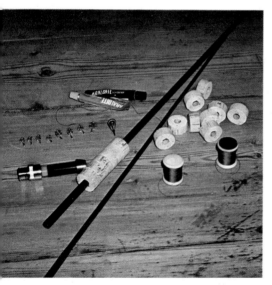

It may be less expensive for you to make up your own rod from a kit. Another advantage is that by placing the rings in various positions on the rod blank, different actions can be obtained. The cork rings are glued to the blank and then formed to the required shape by sandpapering them to make the handle. You will then have a 'custom-built' handle, which will help to make your fishing more enjoyable—another advantage of a kit. The overall saving on the price of a rod could be in the region of 20 per cent or more.

handed rods would be used. And the short brook rods of between 6 and 8ft (1.8 and 2.4m) are more suitable for fishing among cover and foliage, where it would be impossible or at least extremely difficult fishing with a 10ft (3m) rod. Over short distances, a shorter rod is also far more accurate.

Line

The length of a fly-line is usually 30 yards (27.4m). The type of fishing and the prevailing conditions determine the weight of line to be used. Dry-flyfishing on a calm day over short distances can be done with an AFTM 4 or 5 line, but on a blustery day or over longer distances you would need an AFTM 6 or perhaps 7. Longer-distance wet-fly or lure-fishing would require perhaps an AFTM 8 or 10 line, and for salmon an AFTM 9–12 line is normal.

Whether a fly-line sinks or floats does not depend on its weight. Fly-lines are made of plastics for reasons of water resistance and suppleness, and their density can be varied to cause them to sink or float. The core

A short brook rod can be an advantage on small streams.

Matching Rod and Line

Regardless of the type of rod or type of line used, a rapport between tackle and caster will not be reached unless both rod and line are matched to each other. The line must be of sufficient weight to flex the rod properly. Otherwise casting will be impaired. Similarly, good results will certainly not be achieved by over-loading the rod. A line too heavy for the rod will also result in clumsy casting and will break the rod sooner or later. Carbon-fibre rods, however, have a greater tolerance for unevenly matched lines than other rods.

Matching rod and line is a simple matter, because both are sold with AFTM ratings clearly marked (see opposite page). Although the ratings are based on the weight of the fly-line in grains, they apply to rods too, because a particular weight of line or range of lines is recommended for each rod.

inside the plastic coating can also be varied to make a sinking line sink at various speeds, from very slow to very fast. A very fast one will sink at about 6 inches (15cm) per second. The core may be made of lead, or the line may be lead-impregnated.

Fly-lines are tapered in a number of different ways. The taper allows the heaviest part of the line to be in the most desirable position in its length.

A *double-taper* line has its thickest part in the centre, and tapers evenly in both directions to its thinnest points at either end. A *single-taper* line tapers only one way, and after the centre tapers off very much more quickly. The double-taper is useful because it is reversible on the reel

AFTM Ratings

The AFTM scale is a system of classifying fly-lines by weight. Devised by the Association of Fishing Tackle Manufacturers in the United States, it numbers lines from 1 to 12; the heavier the line, the higher the number. Rods are also designated AFTM ratings for matching purposes.

The lines are also coded with letters indicating where the weight is concentrated or how the line is tapered. The following are fairly standard:

DT=double-taper; WF=weight-forward (forward taper); ST=shooting-taper; S=sinking; F=floating; F/S=floating/sinking.

A line coded WF7F would be a weight-forward AFTM 7 floating line.

when one end has worn. For short distances and delicate fly presentation, these two lines are the most popular. Double-taper fly-lines were the first to be used extensively, being a distinct advance on the original level line, which was made of silk and greased to make it float.

The increase in popularity of lake and reservoir flyfishing also inspired an advance in the design of fly-lines. The need for casting greater distances led to the introduction of the weight-forward taper and the shooting taper, more usually called a shooting-head. A *weight-forward taper* fly-line has its thickest part about 5 yards (4.6m) from the forward end, to which it

tapers smoothly. It tapers more quickly towards the rear, the taper ending at about 12 yards (11m). This is an advantage when casting long distances, because it is not necessary to 'aerialize' as much line as with the double-taper, it requires less energy from the caster, and it is subject to less false casting because the thin level line behind the tapered 'belly' shoots easily through the rod rings.

The *shooting-head* is a type of weight-forward line, with the taper condensed into about 12 yards (11m). But instead of being attached to level fly-line, it joins a backing of monofilament nylon, which allows the line to slip even more easily through the

Left: When fishing amongst foliage, the short rod is a definite advantage. By lowering the rod on the final delivery of the cast, the line can be cast to avoid overhanging trees or bushes.

Below: Exaggerated drawings illustrating the different kinds of fly-line taper.

Double taper

Weight-forward taper

Shooting-taper

There are a number of types of reel available for flyfishing. Your choice will probably be governed by cost. Top left: An automatic recovery reel (note the absence of a handle). Top right: A carbon-fibre reel, which has a larger spool and is ideal for shooting-tapers because it eliminates tight coils formed in the backing by small spindles. Bottom left: A multiplier, which revolves the spool several times for each turn of the handle. Bottom right: A single action reel.

rod rings. This, together with its extra lightness, helps to increase casting distances.

Reels

Having the right weight of reel attached to a rod can be an advantage, although much criticism of un-matched reels and rods may well be unfounded. The reel, in effect, is no more than an accessory, and much of the time is only ever used simply to store the line—the actual playing of the fish is often done by stripping the line in by hand. But it would obviously be ridiculous to encumber a short brook rod with a heavy reel. Such rods are usually coupled with a small-diameter reel. This is possible because the shorter distances involved do not require much backing to the line, and the lighter AFTM rated lines used do not take up so much space on the spool as the heavier lines. For longer-distance work, the reel must be capable of holding a full fly-line and at least 50 yards (45m) of monofilament backing, and pre-ferably 100 yards (91m).

In general, the larger the spool of the reel, the fewer tangles you will experience when fishing, because the retrieved line will be in wider coils. This is particularly true of shooting-heads, because the nylon backing tends to stay in coils until it has been stretched, although the braided nylon is better in this respect.

With the heavier rods used in lakes and reservoirs and for salmon, the reels may be heavier without up-setting the balance of the tackle. But to help balance the lighter carbon-fibre rods, carbon-fibre reels are now in production.

Of the types of reel available, the basic single-action reel revolves the line spool once for each turn of the handle. The *multiplying reel* revolves the spool several times for each turn of the handle, and the *automatic reel* recovers line rapidly with the touch of a lever. For beginners, the

Make sure before fishing that your landing net has a long enough handle to cope with conditions on the bank. The one shown above is most popular.

basic reel should be adequate, and is far less expensive.

Leaders

One look at a fly-line is enough to convince even a novice that it cannot be tied direct to a fly. Joining the fly-line to the fly is a length of fine nylon monofilament line called the *leader*. It may be tapered or level, and it may be continuous or have several shorter lengths of nylon ('droppers') attached for fishing a 'team' of flies.

Just as the rod and line are important for casting, and the line for fishing the fly at the right depth, so the leader is important in the presentation of the fly to the fish. Once rod and line have completed their tasks, the leader takes over. If the nylon is too short or too thick, the fish will be aware of the tackle and become alarmed, with the result that it will refuse the fly.

To present a dry fly properly, a knotless tapered leader is ideal, because it will cause the fly to roll out beyond the fly-line. This allows the line to stay behind the fish without alarming it, if presentation is correct.

For wet-flyfishing, a tapered leader may be used with up to four, but more usually three, dropper knots leading off at intervals, allowing a team of wet flies to be fished. This increases the chances of tempting a fish, either because there is a greater likelihood of including the correct pattern or simply because three or four flies in close proximity to each other may appeal to its appetite.

In lure-fishing, presentation is not so important, because usually greater depths are being fished. In this case, all you need for a leader is a length of level nylon taken from a spool.

Care of Tackle

Your tackle will probably be in constant use throughout the season, and it can be quite a chore to clean and maintain it after every outing. But it is worth the trouble. Remember that not only can tackle be expensive, but poorly tended equipment might lose you the fish of a lifetime. You would find it hard to forgive yourself if a really big one got away solely because you failed to carry out an elementary check, say, on your reel.

Some tasks are basic and should be carried out at the start of every fishing expedition. For example, the knot that secures your leader to the fly-line should be tested for strength, and so should the knot that secures the fly-line to the backing.

There are also operations that should be carried out at regular intervals. You should dismantle your reel, clean it with an oily rag, and oil it. If possible, keep it in a case to prevent dirt and grit from reaching the works. You should also inspect the rod rings, and replace them if they are showing signs of wear.

Fly-lines also need attention, even if they are made of plastic or similar material. Remove your fly-line from the reel and clean it with a recommended cleaning agent. At the same time, check the backing for chafing and to ensure that it runs off the reel smoothly.

Taking care of your tackle will give it a longer life and will increase your enjoyment of the use of it. It is best done on returning after each outing, or whenever you feel it is necessary. Wiping the rod (above right) will ensure that grit and abrasive particles are removed. This will help the varnish to last longer and so preserve the rod, a most important point with cane but less so with man-made materials. Dismantling the reel (below right) and wiping it with an oily rag before oiling it will ensure that it operates smoothly and efficiently. This could prevent it jamming or causing a tangle when you are fishing, which in turn could result in losing a fish.

Hooks

Short shank

Medium shank

Long shank

Up-eyed

Barb-less

A fine rainbow trout with a Muddler Minnow fly in the front of its jaw. This is a poor hookhold and may soon loosen.

Both up-eyed and down-eyed hooks are commonly used for flyfishing. Choice of hook depends on which type of fly is being used. The eye of the fly is the part that accepts the leader, which is then knotted accordingly. Whether the hook is up-eyed or down-eyed dictates how the leader rests in relation to the fly.

Dry flies are normally tied on up-eyed hooks, so that the leader rests on the surface of the water without breaking the surface. As a result, it will not sink and drag the dry fly under the surface, a crucial point sometimes.

Wet flies, nymphs, and flies representing other creatures are tied on down-eyed hooks.

Salmon flies, which are in the main larger than the other wet and dry flies, are generally tied on up-eyed hooks. Wet-flyfishing for salmon is generally practised close to the bottom in cold spring weather. So, with the long rod held high, the fly will fish point upwards, with less chance of snagging the bottom.

Shank
The other important characteristic of hooks is the shank. As a rule, either short-shank or medium-shank hooks are used for dry flies and wet flies. But some nymphs are tied on long-shank hooks. Lures and salmon flies are tied on either medium- or long-shank hooks to accommodate the extra dressing usually used to provide bulk and shape.

Size
Hooks are designated by size. Dry flies and nymphs can be tied on a hook as small as a No. 22 or as large as a long-shank 10. Lures and salmon flies usually range from a size 10 long shank, which is small, to a size 2/0 long shank, which is very large and is used for sea fish or larger freshwater fish such as pike.

Knots

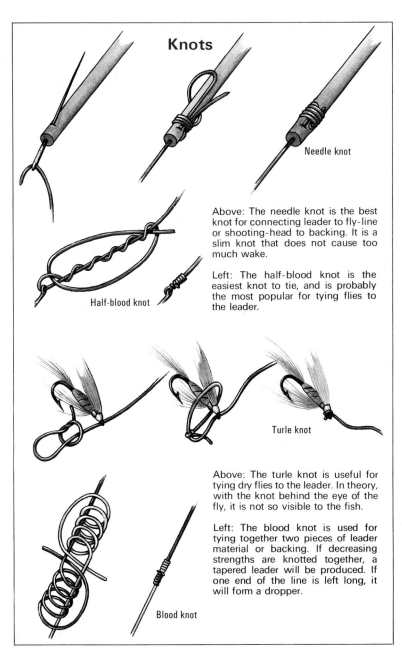

Needle knot

Above: The needle knot is the best knot for connecting leader to fly-line or shooting-head to backing. It is a slim knot that does not cause too much wake.

Left: The half-blood knot is the easiest knot to tie, and is probably the most popular for tying flies to the leader.

Half-blood knot

Turle knot

Above: The turle knot is useful for tying dry flies to the leader. In theory, with the knot behind the eye of the fly, it is not so visible to the fish.

Left: The blood knot is used for tying together two pieces of leader material or backing. If decreasing strengths are knotted together, a tapered leader will be produced. If one end of the line is left long, it will form a dropper.

Blood knot

The Flies

A caddis or large sedge fly, which forms a large part of the trout diet as a hatching fly during summer months and a grub in cooler weather.

One of the most appealing aspects of flyfishing is the great variety of patterns, colours, and shapes of the flies. They range from minute imitations of floating insects (dry flies), to large multicoloured gaudy salmon flies, or the very large flies used for salt-water fishing. Whatever they are, there is a certain delight in producing your own flies. Each fly that you tie is a separate creation of your very own, even though it may be a direct copy of another. Most flies possess a certain style which reflects the tier's individuality.

Another important consideration is that flies you tie yourself work out much cheaper than shop-bought ones, and the quality may also be better. And there is the added attraction of being able to extend your fishing into your own home.

There is an immense amount of enjoyment to be had sitting before your fly-tying vice on an evening shortly before the season starts and

inventing a pattern that looks good enough for a trout to eat. There is then all the anticipation of the following period when you long to be at the waterside to try your new patterns on the fish. At the waterside, you look at the fly in the water to check that it 'swims' correctly, and then you fish with it. Finally, there is an ecstatic thrill when the first fish takes hold of your very own pattern of fly.

Of course, we all tend to forget that after the close season there will be fish in the water that will take almost anything that is offered to them. But then that is the best time to try new patterns if you are a beginner, because of the confidence you will gain in your fly-tying ability.

Tools and Materials
The basic tools required for fly-tying are a vice, hooks, bobbin holder, hackle pliers, scissors, and dubbing needle. The basic tying and fixing materials are wax, thread, and var-

nish. The dressing materials you can use range from feathers, hair, and silks that you can buy in tackle shops to tufts of carpet, hairs from your dog, and so on. If you come across a dead animal or bird in the countryside, check it over to see if there are any feathers or hair that might be useful. Some fly-tiers even breed chickens for their hackles!

As you progress with fly-tying, you will soon find yourself attempting more intricate patterns, so it is worth starting off with a good vice. You will be faced with a wide choice, but go for one that adjusts in as many ways as possible—that is, the most expensive one you can afford.

Several materials have multiple uses. Perhaps the most versatile of all the regular fly-dressing materials is a feather from the centre of the tail of a cock pheasant. This can be used, for example, to make an entire fly, or to build up a thorax on another, or to provide wing cases for a nymph fly. Peacock herl is a similarly versatile feather. These two feathers, together with a good selection of different-coloured hen and cock hackles, will enable you to tie flies to suit almost any situation you will encounter. A

Parts of the Fly

In a typical wet fly (1), the wings are tied sloping back over the hook-shank and the throat hackle does not extend all round the shank. The body is dressed to sink, and more usually ribbed with, or made of, tinsel. The dry flies (2) can be tied with the wings in many positions—e.g. forward sloping or backward sloping, spent or with no wing at all but simply a spun hackle. The hackle always extends a full circle around the hook-shank unless it is tied parachute-style. The body is dressed of a light material or sparsely dressed. A lure (3) is generally much larger than wet or dry flies. It has more in common with the wet flies and is more usually heavily dressed to create an impression of bulk to the fish. Lures are usually fished on sinking lines.

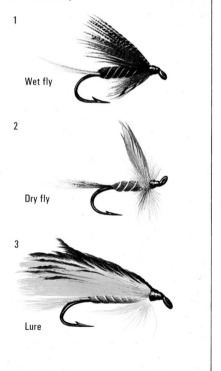

1

Wet fly

2

Dry fly

3

Lure

number of different-coloured seal's furs will increase that range many times over.

Fly-Tying Basics

As with most new skills, when you begin your fly-tying you will experience a number of frustrations for various reasons. But the two most important points are to keep as much pressure on the thread as it will stand without breaking and to leave sufficient room near the eye of the hook to finish off the head.

If you are tying a fly in stages, after each stage take just a couple of turns over the hook to hold the previous stage in place. Let the thread hang down under the weight of the bobbin holder. It is most infuriating, having let go of the thread to prepare a hackle for tying, to see out of the corner of your eye the beautifully spiralled tinsel you have just used to form a body come flying off the hook in a straggly mess.

Another useful hint is that anything required to be in a particular

The equipment needed for tying your own flies can be as varied and as expensive as you care to make it. It is advisable to buy a versatile vice (such as the one shown above), where the head can be angled, turned, or inverted. Many materials can be accumulated, but it is important to keep them as tidy as possible, with a special box or case for containing the kit. A flexible table lamp is essential for such close work, and will help to avoid possible eye-strain.

line above or below the hook shank should be held in place on the shank with finger and thumb, and the thread tying it should be as tight as possible during that stage. Otherwise the material will slip when you tighten up later. This applies mainly to hackles used to form wings or tails and to throat hackles.

Seal's fur and other furry materials have a special way of being tied called 'dubbing'. The principle is that you wax your tying thread well, take a bunch of fur, and with finger and thumb spin it down the thread to form a rope. Then wind the thread on the fly to form the required body or thorax. This is a most effective way of tying because of the translucence of the fur in water.

For nearly all types of flies, the basic methods for starting and tying off are the same. The start and the 'whip finish' are illustrated below. On the following six pages are examples of three typical flies, with step-by-step illustrations and instructions for tying them.

The start of a fly and the finish are basically the same for most flies. In the start (left), the thread is laid along the hook shank and several turns laid back towards the bend until it is firmly anchored. In the so-called 'whip finish' (below), the thread is pulled back along the hook shank and the index and middle fingers used to make at least four turns over it before pulling it tight and cutting it off. Wool has been used for demonstration purposes in the whip finish.

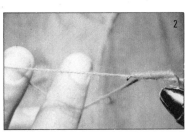

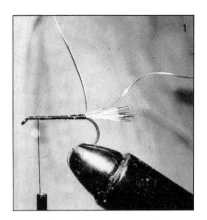

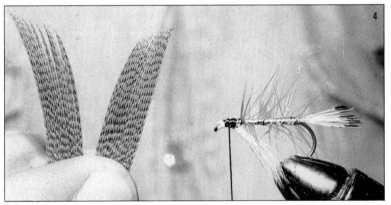

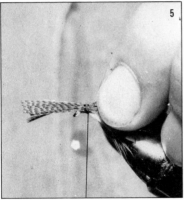

The Dunkeld
(Wet Fly)

The Dunkeld is a traditional wet fly pattern and is an attractor fly. After fixing your hook in the vice, start off your thread and take it to the bend. Tie in a bunch of golden pheasant tippets, a length of flat gold tinsel and a length of oval gold tinsel (1). Take the thread back to the eye, wind the flat tinsel to the eye in touching turns, and secure it. Take an orange cock hackle and tie it in at the eye. Grasping the point in the hackle pliers, wind it in a wide spiral back to the bend (2). Secure the orange hackle with a turn of the oval tinsel, and wind this in the opposite direction to the hackle in a wide spiral up to the eye and tie it in. Tie in a few yellow fibres from a cock hackle to form the throat (3). Snip two bunches of fibres from the bronze feathers of a mallard drake, ensuring that the fibres do not separate, and pair them together (4). Place the wings with the pale sides together on top of the hook shank and, holding them firmly, secure them so that they do not slip round the hook as you tie them in (5). Having secured the wings in place, partially finish off the head and snip off the waste to the wings (6). Finish off the head with a whip finish and varnish it to produce the finished fly (7).

The Dunkeld can be fished at any time of the year and at any depth, although it was first developed for loch-style fishing.

Pheasant-Tail Nymph

The Pheasant-Tail Nymph is a very simple fly to tie and can be produced in many varieties. For instance, the fly may be plain or it may have a variety of different coloured thoraces, and it can be any size you like to tie it. First, select a feather from the centre of the tail of a cock pheasant and strip from it a number of fibres according to the size of the fly to be tied (1). Having already tied in your thread and returned it to the bend of the hook, tie in the tips of the fibres to leave them extending behind the hook (2). Return the thread to about two-thirds towards the eye and leave it there. Twist the fibres together and wind them in touching turns to meet the thread. Secure them with two turns of the thread, but ensure that they are on top of the shank (3). Tie in the coloured wool, which will form the thorax, and return the thread to the eye (4). Wind the wool round the shank to form a round thorax, finishing it at the eye, and tie in and snip off the excess (5). Now take the ends of the fibres which are loose, lay them firmly over the thorax, and take several turns of thread over them (6). Now that the fibres are in place, grip them again and pull firmly (7) to keep them in contact with the thorax before tying them in firmly and snipping off the excess. Finish off the head and varnish it (8).

This is a most versatile fly, best fished on a floating line and retrieved slowly, although a large version could be fished as a fry imitator.

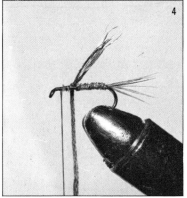

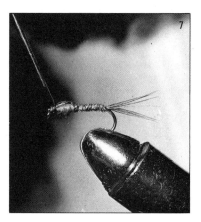

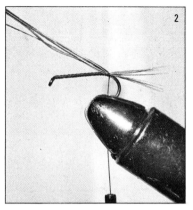

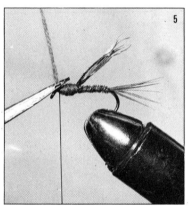

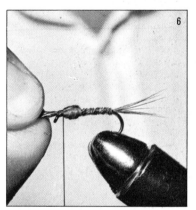

Black Ghost Lure

The Black Ghost is a lure, intended
to attract predatory fish. A simple
lure to tie, it incorporates only
basic materials and techniques.
Start the thread as usual, and leave
it at the bend of the hook. Tie in a
tail of yellow fibres taken from a
cock hackle, a length of oval silver
tinsel, and a length of black
marabou silk (1). Take the tying
thread back to the eye and leave
it there. Take the black silk to the
eye in touching turns, and tie it in.
Then take the tinsel in wide spirals
in the opposite direction to the
silk and tie it in (2). Tie in a bunch
of yellow fibres to form the throat
hackle (3). Take a pair of white
cock hackles and, using the nail of
your thumb against the index
finger, tear off unwanted fibres.
Tie the hackles in with their
natural curves turning inwards (4).
Repeat the process with another
pair of hackles, and ensure that
their curves face towards the first
pair. If the wings extend too far
beyond the bend of the hook, the
fly will not fish properly and the
wings will twist around the hook
shank on casting. Having tied in
both wings (5), trim them off at
the eye and finish off the head
and varnish it (6). If you have
trouble getting the wings to lie on
the hook properly, grip them with
your spare hand between finger
and thumb and hold them as you
would like them to be when
finished. Then take just one or two
turns of thread back towards the
bend, beyond the head already
formed, and finish off the head
properly. Be careful not to upset
the throat hackle when doing so.

The Black Ghost is usually fished
on a sinking line at any time of
the season.

Casting

Whether casting single-handed (left) or double-handed (above) the rod must be gripped firmly.

Casting, like fly-tying, is a special aspect of flyfishing that brings further satisfaction over and above that of catching fish. There is an exquisite pleasure in casting a nice line to a cruising fish that takes the fly as it proceeds on its way. If the cast is made clumsily or inaccurately, though, the fish will either be frightened away or may not even notice the fly.

The secret of accurate and easy casting is in matched tackle. The line must be the right weight for the rod. The weight in flyfishing is concentrated totally in the fly-line, and not in the end-tackle as in coarse or sea fishing. So it is distributed over a fairly long length, and casting is in some respects like wielding a whip.

The casting operation entails more than just 'throwing' the line and fly into or onto the water. A certain amount of 'false-casting' is necessary to get the rod working, and this usually involves at least two back and forward casts—back, forward, back, forward and onto the water.

The best conditions in which to begin casting for the first time are with a fairly light breeze blowing from behind or from the side away from your casting arm. You can make a simple start by laying a short length of line on the water and picking it up smartly so that if flies out behind you. Repeat the movement several times to help you gain the feel of the rod working with the line loaded. The basic casting techniques are explained and illustrated on the following pages (42–45), as well as the 'double haul' (page 46), used for achieving extra distance, and retrieving (page 47).

When beginning casting as a novice, do not strive for distance. Simply concentrate on achieving the rhythm required, and once you do so every other aspect will fall into place.

The finer points, and very important ones to remember, are (1) to keep the rod roughly between the positions corresponding to 10 and 1 on a clock; (2) when releasing line, to imagine a horizontal line level with the point of your rod-tip and try to keep the fly-line as high as this imaginary line; and (3) to keep your arm tucked well into your side and

never let your wrist turn away from a straight line with your arm.

The simple casting action does not take long to accomplish. But, of course, it takes years of practice to master, say, the techniques required to make a dry fly land as a natural one would, or to cast in difficult conditions, such as from under trees or with obstacles fore and aft. Learning to cast left-handed (if you are right-handed) and backhanded will give you additional scope in difficult conditions.

Above: The Spey cast is the method used to cast the farthest possible distance without the line actually extending behind the rod.

Below left: A fish's 'window', or angle of vision through the surface, is restricted to an angle of about 97° So theoretically, a fish can see more above the surface the lower it is in the water. Below: A trout's angle of vision underwater is 330° when using its eyes independently, but only 30° when it focuses them on an object.

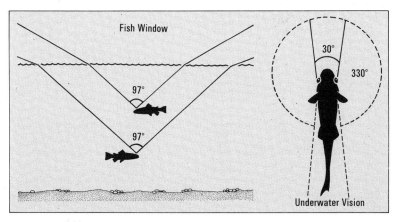

The rod has not yet started to flex properly as the cast is only just beginning (1). It is important that the rod is stopped at '1 o'clock'. The line is brought behind in a curve, and time is given for it to straighten before the forward cast is made (2). When the back-cast has straightened, the rod is pushed forward with a rigid wrist in order to flex the rod as it is doing here (3). The rod is then stopped while the line comes from behind, and there is a pause before the next back-cast. The line is then allowed to come forward in a curve (4) and extend as far beyond the rod

as is possible without actually losing all of its momentum. Then, still maintaining a rigid wrist, the rod is brought back (5) in preparation for the next back-cast. If the wrist is not rigid, it will allow the rod to move out of line, which will cause it to flex insufficiently. And if the back-cast or forward cast is begun before the line has straightened, or too long after it has done so, there will not be sufficient weight created by the line to flex the rod. With each forward cast, line has been released and the rod can now be seen to be flexing

(contd. over)

on the back cast (6).
On the beginning
of the forward cast, the
rod is now obviously
doing more of the work
and can be felt to be
doing so. The rod is
actually on its way
through the beginning of
the forward cast (7) and
will be stopped at
'10 o'clock' before the
pause. This will allow the
line to straighten out in
front before more line is
released and the next
back-cast started. The line
is again curving forward
before straightening on
the forward cast (8). The
rod has already flexed and
the momentum it created

in doing so has been imparted to the line. Upon the line straightening, the left hand will release more line and the back-cast will begin again before the line falls (9). To complete the cast, the rod is lowered on the last forward cast and the line released completely by the left hand, so that it is free to fly forward propelled by the rod movement (10).

Actual presentation of the line is fully dependent on the final position of the rod at the final forward cast. Here, with a wind coming from the side, the presentation will be lighter than with a rod held higher. With a following wind, a rod held higher would result in the cast travelling farther, but landing more heavily on the water. When casting into a wind, a very firm punch on the final delivery and a low rod-tip will produce a tighter loop, which will travel farther into the wind than a wide loop. At all times, you should ensure that while the rod is going through the casting motions it is working as much as possible.

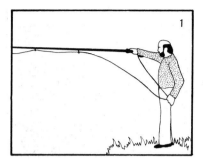

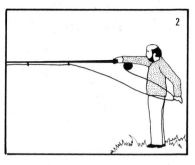

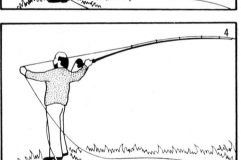

The Double Haul

The double haul is an advanced technique used to gain extra distance. This is done by using the left hand in synchronization with the rod to increase the speed of the line. The forward cast is made and the line extended (1). The line has straightened and the left hand pulls sharply on it as the rod is starting to come back at the beginning of the back-cast (2). The rod is at its farthest limit on the back-cast, and the left hand is ready to haul again (3). The left hand has just started to haul, and the flexing of the rod can be seen (4). On the final delivery, the rod is pushed forward at the same time as the left hand hauls, as before, but as the line straightens it is released. The open left hand can be seen (5) with the loose line flying from the ground as it travels forward.

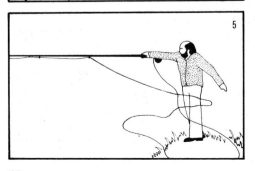

Retrieving

In retrieving, the fly-line is left to lie on the ground or the water where it falls, or to gather in some suitable receptacle such as a line tray.

There are two basic rules relating to the rod when you are retrieving: (1) with a floating line, hold it more or less horizontal; (2) with a sinking line, point it down the line.

To hold the line, trap it under tension against the cork rod handle with your forefinger. With your free hand, retrieve the line either by stripping it with a long pull and repeating until sufficient line has been recovered, or by using the figure-of-eight method illustrated below.

Use the forefinger trapping the line as a sort of clutch, applying momentary extra pressure to hook a taking fish and easing it to allow the fish to take line if necessary. Never clamp the line rigidly to the rod, or the leader or hook may be broken.

In the retrieve, which is known as 'stripping', the line is trapped between rod handle and forefinger (1). The left hand grips the line near the right hand and keeps extending fully (2).

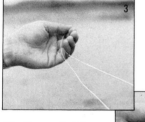

The figure-of-eight retrieve maintains constant movement of the fly. The forefinger and thumb are used to grip the line (3). The remaining fingers gather in the line to the palm of the hand (4), and the line is then trapped with the index finger and thumb and the movement repeated until the retrieve has been completed (5).

Current

B

C

Hooking, Playing, and Landing

To the beginner, once a fish has taken a fly, that might seem the end of the matter and the rest could be left to take care of itself. But the hooking, playing, and landing of a fish are steps that require experience to master. Your quarry can escape at any time after it has taken your offering, and it is particularly frustrating if it gets away as you are about to land it. And if you are faced with playing and landing a big one before you have gained sufficient practice, it can be nerve-racking and eventually disappointing.

Somewhere in these three stages is the origin of all those stories of the 'big one that got away' about which anglers are constantly teased. My own experience has been that the best fish often do get away.

Hooking

The best penetration can be achieved with the sharpest hooks, so always ensure that your hooks are as sharp as possible. Check the point regularly in case you have blunted it on something when casting or retrieving.

There is rarely any real need to 'strike' unless you see a fish take your fly but have not felt it. If you feel the fish take, it is usually because the line has tightened, and you can set the hook simply by firmly raising the rod-tip. If you only see the fish take, strike with a smart action of the rod, which will pull the hook backwards into the fish's mouth and not forwards out of it. All of the time your line should be trapped by your forefinger against the rod handle, but be ready to release it slightly if the

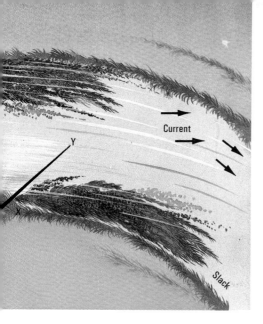

A fish will use the current to the best of its ability when fighting. In this situation, hold the rod hard over at position 'A-B' to prevent the hooked fish reaching the weed bed in mid-stream, or the flotsam between the trees. The same position may also be used to prevent it reaching the overhanging trees and far weed bed. Use rod position 'X-Y' if the fish turns downstream to keep it from the subsurface weeds on either bank. Net fish from position C.

fish is too powerful to hold. Use as much force as you can exert without breaking the leader in order to set the hook as deep as possible over the barb.

Different fish take the fly in different ways. As a rule of thumb, you would usually expect predators to take the fly with a rush, and non-predators to take it gently. But you will experience all sorts of different takes, and the best way to be ready to deal with them all is by maximum concentration on the line and leader if it is visible.

Playing

Again, you will experience a great variation in the way fish behave once you have hooked them. So you still need to maintain the utmost concentration. Be ready to counter every move the fish might make in an effort to rid itself of the restraining force you have introduced to it. Hooked fish immediately become very wild, and the tactic of countering all moves

bewilders them and makes them easier to net.

One trait peculiar to my own fishing is that I like to have a look at the fish as soon as possible—for two reasons. The first is to see how big it is and what it is, and the second to see where it is hooked. If it is a large fish hooked in the scissors, or gristle of the mouth, I feel more relaxed than if it is hooked in the point of the jaw or a lesser hook hold. If you want to

A fish securely hooked in the scissors. This is probably the most secure place in which to hook a fish.

49

try this tactic, immediately you hook the fish aim to bring it near you.

When playing a fish, never give it any slack line unless the circumstances are exceptional. This applies particularly if you see that your fish might be loosely hooked in the point of the mouth. You have everything to gain by trying to end the battle as quickly as possible, because to prolong it with a poor hook hold is almost certainly to lose your fish.

Instead of simply holding your rod as high as possible all the time and holding on, try to confuse the fish by using force from different angles. For instance, if the fish resists a high rod and dives and swims with its tail up, turn the rod to a horizontal position and use pressure that way. The fish will then be turned on its side and forced to employ other tactics. Try to keep its head up as much as possible. When a strong fish has its head down and you are trying to pull it backwards, it seems a formidable opponent. But exert a pull from the side and it is a different matter.

You should always take into consideration any restrictions to rod

Playing the Fish

To net a fish properly is not always a simple matter. When you feel sure that the fish is tiring, have the net ready and, holding the rod high, bring the fish towards you (1). If the fish is not ready for netting and you attempt to do so too early, it will shy away from the net (2). However, continued pressure will bring it back to the net if the hook holds. The fish

movement, such as bank vegetation or boat partners. But if you remember this before you start fishing, you can make sure that you have as much freedom of movement as possible.

If your fish comes to the surface and starts to thrash, do not hold the rod high and just hope that it stays on. Turn the rod to the horizontal position, and the fish will go down again and invariably go off on a run. In this event, hold the rod high and keep the line out of the water as much as possible in order to maintain direct contact and reduce water resistance to the line.

If the fish leaps from the water, release the line momentarily and lower the rod-tip immediately. Otherwise, as the fish falls back in the water, it might fall on the leader or at a point farther from you, and by twisting its body exert sufficient sudden pressure to snap the leader in either case.

Of course, there are always the fish that prove the exception to the rule. You may well find when you hook a fish that it turns out to be a 'brute' that immediately and unstoppably makes for a weed bed or rock, and

will probably 'kite' across in front of you (3), but by maintaining pressure you can turn it towards the net and hold its head up (4). You then

draw the fish over the sunken net (5), and, as soon as it is within the rim, lift the net and engulf the fish in it, preventing any further attempts to swim off. A deep landing net (6) is an asset, because this will render it impossible for the fish to throw itself out, as it might do in a shallow net.

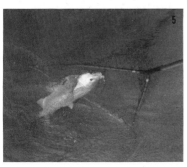

Although the fish here is thrashing the water, it has been engulfed in the net and is safely netted. The angler has released the tension on the line, and lowered his rod so that the fish is not given any possible leverage.

secures itself there with no intention of moving. In this case, try exerting a constant pressure to the maximum that your leader will stand, and hope that it is enough to move the fish. If it becomes evident that the fish is not going to move, try repeated short, hard pulls, and if these do not work try waiting a while to see if the fish will move of its own accord. If not, lay the rod down and then keep pulling at the line with your hands until either the leader breaks or the fish comes away. If you can wade in to it, you might be able to net it out or push it from the snag.

In most cases, sidestrain will prevent your fish from doing what it wants to do. But you must concentrate on its every movement, and once it starts coming up through the water, keep it moving in case you can get its head out of the water and then attempt to land it.

Landing

Before you start the netting operation, make sure that the net is well submerged. Once your fish is on the surface, on its side with its head held out by the leader, push the net forward without touching the fish. Draw the fish over it and lift the net so that the fish is engulfed. If the fish is too long for the net, make sure that its head and shoulders will go in

and then lift the net up. The rest will follow.

Remember, though, even at this stage of the proceedings stealth is still important. Try to crouch out of sight of the fish. And always avoid any unnecessary movement. An alarmed fish at the net is often a lost fish.

If you give the fish a chance to lever against the rim of the net with its tail, it will be off again, and may even break the leader. If you thrust the net at a fish, it will become alarmed and use all its remaining energy in a bid to wrench itself free from the hook. Losing a fish at this stage is particularly frustrating.

Be very careful, too, of any droppers you may be using, because if these catch in the net, and the fish has been netted or is still swimming, they could cause problems (see page 62).

Having netted your fish, always ensure that it is dealt with immediately. If you intend to keep it, then use the priest straight away before extracting the hook. And if you are returning it, extract the hook with the minimum of handling and allow it to swim off. Always wet your hands before handling fish you intend to return. If you follow these procedures, the fish will be spared unnecessary suffering.

Landing and Unhooking

An adequate landing net is essential in a boat. The angler's net (below) is of excellent depth, but the fairly short handle means that the fish could get close to the boat before it can be netted. If the fish is to be returned, it may free itself if the fly is held (below left). It need not then be handled. If the hook is embedded firmly in the fish's mouth or is not easily accessible, a pair of artery forceps can prove invaluable (bottom left). Once the fish has been killed it can be weighed on a spring balance. If it is not to be killed, the landing net mesh can be used.

Choice of Method

There are three distinct methods of flyfishing – wet, dry, and nymph – and the line may be floating or sunk. On any particular day, and for any specific set of conditions, the first decision to be made upon arrival at the waterside is the method to be used.

There are several factors that affect the choice of method: the weather, the apparent presence or absence of fish, the depth and nature of the water, and whether there are any snags or obstructions in the water. Fortunately for the flyfisher, though, there is a practical method for fishing every water.

Bright sunshine is usually a hindrance whatever method of flyfishing is used, but is especially so when fishing near the surface in smooth water. As a rule, cloudy and dull weather is better for fishing at or near the surface, because the shadow of the line is not so apparent to the fish. On the other hand, rain can make dry-flyfishing impossible, because the floating fly would be repeatedly sunk by bombarding raindrops. In certain

circumstances, however, it may be possible to cast to rising fish and cover them before the fly is sunk.

The first thing to look for when surveying the water is rising fish. If the fish are rising, it is difficult to resist fishing for them, and a floating line with a dry fly or near-surface nymph is the obvious choice. If no fish are rising or showing, then a sinking fly must be considered, either a wet fly or a nymph.

One of the greatest problems in flyfishing running water is floods, recent or present, that have introduced mud to the water and coloured it. Not only does this impair the fishes' vision, but it also makes them less inclined to feed normally. So unless the flyfisher is fully conversant with the contours of the water, he will need a great deal of diligence to produce fish, as well as a certain amount of luck.

If the water is boulder-strewn or weedy, sunk-line fishing can be very difficult. The line will keep getting snagged, and the cast must be ex-

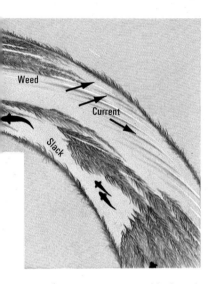

invariably the choice. Wet flies and nymphs may also be fished on a floating line, and this combination should be used if the water is not deep or is infested with snags not far beneath the surface. But for a wide, deep water, where it looks as if the fish are lying deep, a sunk line with nymphs and wet flies is preferable.

A floating line can be fished from upstream or downstream, but a sinking line can be practically fished only downstream, unless the current is very slow. In every case, the leader should be as long as is reasonably manageable, because thick fly-line is more easily visible and causes greater disturbance. But, of course, if the leader is too long, a heavy fly can get snagged on the bottom.

tremely accurate to avoid the obstructions. But in shallow water, fish tend to accumulate in areas where there are weeds and snags, and a short drift with a dry fly should produce results. Such waters are usually fast-flowing, with broken surfaces, so line shadow is no great problem. And as the fly is moving fast, the fish do not have time to inspect it properly. If the same type of water is deep, then it may be possible to fish a sunken line (usually wet fly or lure), at a depth judged to ride just above the snags.

Line and Leader
Fishing dry fly on a sunk line is obviously not the way to keep the fly afloat, so a floating line is almost

Dry, Wet, and Nymph
The methods of fishing dry fly, wet fly, or nymph are gone into in greater detail in the following chapters, and the choice of fly is dealt with also in the chapters on the various fish. With care, all three methods can be combined. Using a floating line, it is possible to fish a dry fly, wet fly, and nymph on the same leader. Any number of combinations can be fished, so long as the nymph is at the opposite end of the leader to the dry fly, more usually at the point (see the diagram of the 'dropper', on page 62). If you need to fish the nymph high in the water, the dry fly should be fished on the point, in order to keep the leader high.

55

Dry Fly

An artificial mayfly floats on the water surface. Notice the shadow created by the line, which is also floating. It would be less noticeable if it was under the surface film.

A dry fly is an artificial fly designed to float on the surface of the water and entice a fish that is feeding on floating insects. Dry-flyfishing can be the most exciting of all the methods, because you are constantly aware of what is happening to the fly, and you can actually see the fish being duped into taking it. A vast thrill of expectation accompanies every drift over a rising fish with a dry fly.

Choice of Fly

When there is an abundance of any particular fly-life (known as a 'hatch') and fish are rising, it may be a safe assumption that the fish are feeding on those flies. Flies that induce fish to rise in this way include the mayfly, sedges, midges, hawthorn flies, and olives. All of these are represented by their own appropriately named imitation. So, unless the variations are very numerous, choosing a pattern is no problem.

Sometimes you will see fish rising without the apparent presence of flies. This could be because they are feeding on nymphs coming up to hatch or on a fly so small that it cannot be seen at the point the fish takes it. With no clues as to what the fish are feeding on, it is usually a good plan to begin fishing over rising fish with conventional, small dry-fly patterns, such as Tup's Indispensable, Black Gnat, Grey Duster, or a pattern to represent one of the flies known as olives.

If a fish is rising but is continually ignoring the artificial offering, it may be because it is wary. You might try reducing the diameter of the leader, as this will make it less apparent. Or it may be that the fly is the wrong colour or too large, or both. Simple observation may provide the answer to this, but more usually you will have to resort to trial and error.

If fish are not rising, 'flogging' the water could well prove quite fruitless. In this case, it might be better to consider a sunk line and use wet flies.

Preparing Fly and Leader

To make sure the fly will float, you need to apply a specially prepared solution, or *floatant*. Sprayed or brushed on to the fly, the floatant aids its buoyancy.

It is important that the first few inches of leader attached to the fly does not float in the surface film. Otherwise, on inspecting the fly, the fish becomes immediately aware of the leader's presence and will deduce that all is not well. As a result, it will become alarmed and stop rising. It might even bolt from its lie and alarm all the other fish in the course of its journey. To avoid this, you can rub a specially prepared compound on the first few inches of the leader to make it sink, or even use plain mud from the river bank. Rubbing the rest of the leader in the same way is used to eliminate 'glitter', a problem that can occur with a new leader—the highly polished surface reflects light and again might alarm the fish.

The Lie

In running water, fish take up a station in the current known as a *lie*. A fish will feed from its lie, content to let the current carry its food to it, without the need to use up precious energy fighting the current. As a result, it is safe to assume that a fish rising from a particular place will probably continue to do so.

Even if a fish becomes alarmed, for whatever reason, it will usually start to rise again eventually at the same place. It should accordingly be 'rested' in order to induce it to do so. But it would be wise, later, to try to tempt it with a different fly, unless it is obvious that it is preoccupied with a particular kind of food.

Drag

The biggest problem that the dry-flyfisher has to contend with is known as *drag*. This is an effect created by varying current speeds or by snags, which affect the line in such a way that it pulls (or drags) the dry fly across the current instead of allowing it to float down naturally at the same speed as that of the current. In the main this unnatural motion of the fly tends to alarm fish, although there will always be the odd fish that will immediately take a dragging fly when it has refused it previously.

Left: With a line cast straight across, the fly is dragged from X to Y, creating a surface disturbance and alarming the fish.
Below: To avoid drag, cast direct from A for fish F_1; from B with a snaky line for F_2; and from C for F_3.

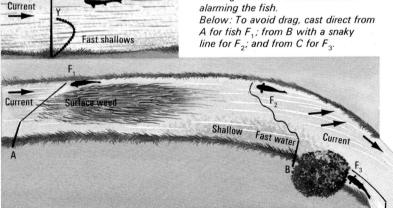

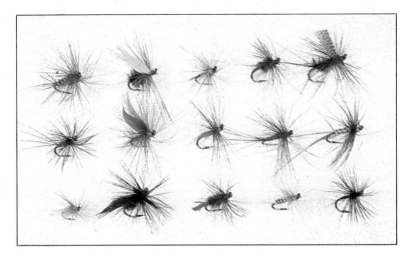

Drag results when a fish is being fished to on the far side of the water, or if the current it is feeding in is faster or slower than that nearest the flyfisher. The fly-line will either be slowed down or speeded up, and line and fly find themselves travelling at different speeds.

There are two solutions to drag caused in this way. One is to be so accurate with the cast that the fly lands almost on the fish's nose and is either taken or has passed it before drag occurs. The other is to make a cast that creates sufficient slack in the fly-line to obviate the effect of the current. In this way, the waves in the line are taken up by the current and drag does not reach the fly until after the rising fish has been covered. Drag may also be avoided, of course, by covering the fish from a different position. But this may not always be possible.

Others factors that cause drag are obstructions or surface weed between the flyfisher and the fish. These catch the fly-line and create the same effect as an adverse current. Usually the

A selection of typical dry flies. They are designed with characteristics to allow them to float — lightweight hooks, lightly dressed bodies, and spun hackles to keep as much of the body as possible in the surface film. The large wings allow the fly to float gently down onto the water after the cast is made, and will not puncture the surface film.

answer is to take up a position upstream of the fish, and so avoid the obstruction. Another way is to cast a longer line, so that when it catches the obstruction or weed there is still sufficient line to reach the fish without drag. Either way, there is an advantage in that the fly may reach the fish before the leader, reducing the chances of alarming it. But offset against this is that in both instances, unless the line can be 'flipped' over the obstruction, the fly and line are retrieved dangerously near to the fish, and this will usually disturb it.

Accuracy and Timing
Casting to fish that are actually lying under or against obstructions such

as overhanging trees, trailing branches, or roots is, paradoxically, usually more straightforward. This is because you have no choice but to make your cast so precise that drag and retrieve do not come into it. The sole factor is accuracy.

The length of time you allow the fly to drift over the fish (if not taken) is a matter of judgement relating to the water. It should be far enough in front of the rising fish to allow it as little time as possible for inspection—although a leisurely rising fish will require more time than a fish 'slashing' at the flies—and it should travel far enough downstream of the fish (if not taken) to be lifted off the water without disturbing the fish. Remember, though, if the fish does take the fly, an instant-reaction strike will simply pull the fly out of its mouth. It should be given sufficient time to turn back down before the strike is made.

Effect of Wind

A downstream wind is a problem to the dry-flyfisher. The only solutions are to find sheltered positions, or a stretch of river that winds differently, or to try to cast more across stream, hoping that the ripple created by the wind will hide line disturbances.

An upstream wind of reasonable proportions, however, is a definite advantage, because it helps to roll the fly ahead of the line.

Dapping on an Irish lough. Dapping involves using either live or artificial flies, such as mayflies or daddy-long-legs, attaching them to the leader and allowing them to be blown in front of the boat as a wind-blown insect would be naturally. Specially made lightweight lines known as 'blow-lines' are used.
Inset left: A cluster of mayflies on a branch prior to laying their eggs in the water.

Wet Fly

In wet-flyfishing, you are attempting to imitate flies or other fauna that are beneath the surface or using an attractor fly to arouse the fishes' aggressive instincts or a lure to imitate a small fish. There is also a choice of line—floating or sinking—depending on whether you are fishing near the surface or deep down, upstream or across.

If there are no obvious signs of fish, you must look for them. This entails a systematic search of the water by casting or by fishing to likely lies. It is important to keep the line reasonably tight to the rod tip, because you will not see the fish take the fly unless it creates subsurface water disturbance as it turns away with it. You will have to watch the leader and/or the line carefully, and you may have to rely on the feel of it to indicate what is happening to the fly.

For upstream fishing or for fishing close to the surface or in restricted areas, a floating line is the best choice. But for deep fishing in wide waters, a sinking line is preferable. When fishing very deep, you may require a fast sinking line to get the fly to the bottom quickly. On the other hand, it is possible to fish just sub-surface with a very slow sinking line.

Floating Line
The sight of fish breaking water with their backs (bulging) or creating swirls as they turn under water is a

A selection of wet flies used in traditional loch-style fishing.

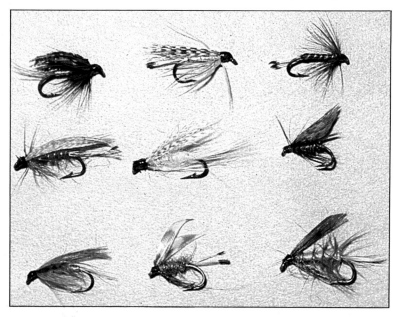

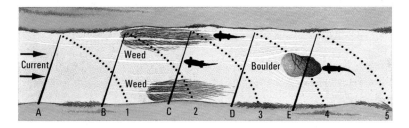

Fishing the downstream wet fly. Move downstream, casting from A, B, C, D, and E, and retrieving when the flies reach positions 1, 2, 3, 4, and 5, respectively. A fish may be covered more than once.

sign that they are feeding just beneath the surface. If this is the case, or if casting space is restricted, or if there are lies that are best covered from a downstream position, you should cast upstream with a floating line. In this way, the angler is out of the line of sight of the fish and they are covered by the flies and not the fly-line. Keep pace with the flies while retrieving. Watch the tip of the fly-line or the floating part of the leader, because any deviation from normal movement could mean that the fish has taken before you even feel it. That is the time to strike.

Drag in wet-flyfishing is not the problem it is in dry fly, because the flies do not create surface disturbance. It is not unusual for a drowning or hatching fly to attempt to reach the surface, so any extra movement on the part of the fly will not arouse the fish's suspicions. But, of course, with a floating line you must still be careful not to create any surface disturbance that will alarm the fish.

As the line is usually at an acute angle upstream, there is little point in allowing the flies to fish on downstream. You will find that fish do not often hook themselves when you are fishing from an upstream position. This is because the hook is pulled back into the fish's mouth when you are fishing from downstream, by a strike or by current

pressure on the line, but is pulled out when the line angles downstream. A strike can be made as soon as you notice any movement of the leader or line, when the fly is upstream or across.

Casting Across Current
When systematically searching the water from upstream, you should take up a position on the bank and make a long cast square across the current. Hold the fly-line tight until the current has brought the fly or flies below that position. Then retrieve the line and make a similar cast, perhaps longer or shorter, until satisfied that no taking fish have been covered. Then take a step or two downstream, adopting the same procedure.

The likeliest time for a fish to take in this sequence is as a bow is introduced into the line by the current. This results in a sudden speeding up of the fly, and causes the fish to lunge at it in an attempt to arrest its escape. The take might show merely as the line stopping and then moving forward quickly for as little as a couple of inches. Or it might be

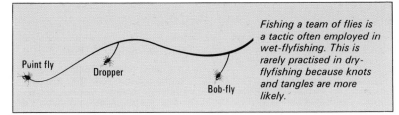

Fishing a team of flies is a tactic often employed in wet-flyfishing. This is rarely practised in dry-flyfishing because knots and tangles are more likely.

Puint fly

Dropper

Bob-fly

a full-blooded take, with the fish firmly hooking itself and wrenching at the rod tip. In either case, you must raise the rod tip sharply to establish instant contact with the fish. This is not a hard and fast rule, though, as there will always be the occasional fish that takes a fly as it is being retrieved upstream and causing a wake.

Sinking Line

A sinking line is likely to prove more efficient on wide, deep waters or waters that are exceptionally deep or fast. Another advantage of the sunk line is that it enables you to reach the larger fish that tend to stay near the bottom. At certain times on hot, bright days, most fish will anyway be lying deeper, and although a fish might not be feeding it could well react to a fly speeding past its nose.

But because you are usually unable to see the line, fishing upstream is more difficult. The accepted method of fishing a sunk line upstream is exactly the same as for searching the water with a floating line. You feel, rather than see, the fish take the fly, holding the line tightly in your hand. The extra pressure brought onto the line by the current means that a fish may easily hook itself. A long rod and a short line work best.

In slack water, you do not have to worry about the direction of the current. The fish are used to seeing food tossed around, and a careful retrieve can produce results.

Fly Teams

When fish are lying deep and not feeding, fly selection may not be as important as when they are pre-occupied. It may be more practicable, depending on the state of the water, to fish just one fly. But fishing a team of three on the leader can be just as easy, and, if they are teamed correctly, will give you more chance of catching fish.

In a team of flies, the fly at the end of the leader is called the *point fly*, the fly in the centre the *dropper*, and the one nearest the fly-line the *bob-fly* (because in still waters it bobs through the waves).

Somewhere on the leader there should be an attractor fly, such as a Dunkeld or a Butcher, and this is usually positioned as the dropper or the bob-fly. The point fly should be more lightly dressed than the other two, and a March Brown, Woodcock and Green, or Mallard and Claret are ideal. The dropper or bob-fly (depending on where the attractor is fished) should be more heavily dressed, say an Invicta or a Wickham's Fancy. The reasoning is that if the imitator flies prove to be interesting to the fish, it will take them. And if it ignores them and then sees the attractor and inspects it, it will either take that fly or the imitator

When and How to Wade

The first rule about wading is that it should be practised sparingly, and then only when absolutely necessary. Wading may be used to get away from a bank where the backcast might get caught up, or to avoid obstructions in the water, such as boulders or rubbish.

But wading is an intrusion into the water. Wading feet stir up the silt on the bottom, crushing insects on which fish feed and dislodging eggs before they are hatched. Unnecessary wading is inconsiderate towards other fly-fishers, too, because it alerts the quarry, giving the fish an awareness of their human predators. For these

reasons, and because it might be dangerous, wading is prohibited in many waters.

If wading is essential, it should be done, usually, on clean bottoms, and with extra care in rocky, strong-flowing rivers—as much for safety's sake as for conservation, and never directly upstream of fish. Always walk gently, feeling the way before placing all the weight on the leading foot. You can use a wading stick or landing-net handle for balance. For wading over an unsure bottom, especially in rough waters, make sure the soles of your waders are studded.

that suddenly appears in front of it as an instant reaction.

More than three flies can be fished as a team, but you have to weigh the disadvantages against the advantages. The more flies there are on the leader, the greater are the chances of tangles. And a jumble of flies suddenly arriving in front of a fish might arouse its suspicions or confuse it.

Changing Tactics

If, for one reason or another, a sinking line is not the line to fish but fishing at depth is still necessary, the solution may be to fish a weighted fly upstream on a floating line. But if the fish are feeding, or thought to be feeding, on nymphs or water insects, the answer is to change tactics and fish with nymphs.

Nymphing

The succulent damsel-fly nymph plays an important part in the diet of most species of fish.

Flyfishers use the term *nymph* to embrace virtually all forms of underwater insect life. This ranges from true water-bred insects that live underwater until they rise to the surface and hatch as flies, to the water beetles, shrimps, and leeches, which spend their entire lives in water.

As these forms of underwater life are always present, the fish are more often inclined to feed beneath the surface and ignore what is happening above. They may be lying in weedy, shallow water feeding on corixae, snails, or shrimps, or they may be taking the nymphs or pupae (in the case, for example, of midges and sedge flies) that are trying to reach the surface where they will hatch. In any event, the absence of fish feeding on any surface food is an indication that the fish are feeding elsewhere. And if there is no sign of fish anywhere, the answer may be to forsake dry fly and wet fly and try nymphs.

At certain times of the day, particularly early morning and late evening, fish may be bulging or swirling, and it is possible that they are taking nymphs on their way to the surface. It is essential to determine at what depth the fish are feeding,

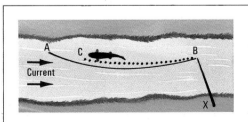

Casting to an upstream nymph. Cast from position X, and no closer. The distance from A to fish should be less than leader length. Retrieve fly at B, but if unsuccessful, try retrieving at C to 'induce' the take.

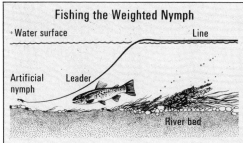

Fishing the Weighted Nymph

Water surface · Line

Artificial nymph · Leader

River bed

To tempt fish feeding near the river bed, use a weighted nymph and allow it to trundle along the bottom. You will recognize a take by the line twitching or stopping, indicating that the fish has the fly confidently. All you need do then is tighten the line.

because, if they are taking hatching nymphs, they could be anywhere between the bottom and the surface.

The same basic principles apply to nymph-fishing, or nymphing, as to wet-flyfishing. Nymphs can be fished singly or in teams, or on floating lines or sinking lines. And the same factors are taken into consideration when deciding how to fish them. The flies, of course, are different.

Choice of Fly

Your basic choices of fly when fish are thought to be chasing hatching nymphs should be olives, browns, blacks, or greys. If none of these produces results, you will again have to resort to trial and error—unless there are signs that point to the use of a particular fly. For example, if sedge flies are present in large quantities but no fish are rising to them, it would be worth trying a sedge pupa imitation. For even if the fish are not feeding on them, they will at least have become used to seeing them in the water. And such a fly brought close to a fish must stand a good chance of being taken. The same principle applies to midges, olives, mayflies, and many more.

If no flies are hatching and the water is completely undisturbed, a good fly to start with would be an imitation of a shrimp, corixa, or snail. It is best to use a weighted version, and to start by fishing the deeper pools, unless you can see fish lying deep in other parts.

These large dark olive nymphs are part of a large family of Ephemerids (short-lived flies), which are also important to most species of fish.

Fishing the Weighted Fly

To fish the deeper water with a weighted fly is perhaps the simplest and most effective method available to nymph-fishers on running water. You need a slightly longer leader than usual, in conjunction with a floating

Opposite: A fluorescent line enables the angler to see the slightest indication that a fish has taken the fly.

A selection of nymphs that would prove useful to either the still-water or stream angler. They include attractors and imitators.

line. You should aim to put the fly in the water well upstream of where you think the fish are lying. This gives the fly time to sink to the required level, and perhaps even to trundle along the bottom. It also means that the fly-line will travel on downstream while the fly is sinking, with the result that at some point the fly is very much in contact with the line. All you have to do then is ensure that the rod has good contact with the line, and so also with the fly. The takes are always obvious and pro-nounced, with a definite twitch of the forward part of the line or leader. Tightening the line firmly usually produces a fish hooked.

If the water has no deep holes, you will have to search it in the same way as with other forms of flyfishing. But if you can see clumps of bottom weed, with clean stretches of bottom between, rolling a fly along the clear parts could bring a fish rushing out of the weeds to take it—a surprising and thrilling experience.

Casting to a Feeding Fish

One of the great joys of flyfishing is to be able to cast to a bottom-feeding fish. You will often spot a fish lying at or near the bottom of a stretch of water, perhaps darting left and right and showing the white of its mouth (which means that it is intercepting food). If the bottom is clean for some distance around, it is likely to be feeding not on snails or shrimps, but on nymphs. At such times, a good fly to start with would be a Pheasant Tail, perhaps one with a coloured

thorax so that it is visible from the bank.

Cast the fly upstream of the fish, and far enough to allow it to sink to the appropriate depth. To do so you might have to create slack in the leader, because a fly-line suddenly alighting over the fish would alarm it. As the fly drifts down to it, you will see the fish's fins start to move more rapidly, as if it is winding up its tail. This is because the strokes are shorter and more frequent—more like a vibration than the previous lazy waggle. As it moves slightly, the white of its mouth becomes visible, and the fly suddenly disappears from view. This is the moment to strike.

It can be as easy as that—but it can be a very different story. The fish might simply move to one side and allow the fly to pass. This is the time to be careful, because it will have ignored the fly for a reason. It has probably seen a similar fly before, and senses that danger is at hand. It

67

should be rested for several minutes while another fly is tied on, preferably a smaller one with a different pattern.

If the fish shows interest but refuses the fly, it is not because it is alarmed or suspicious. There is probably a fault with presentation or pattern. Bringing the fly right onto the fish's nose could effect a take, but you might have to use a drabber or a brighter fly, or a smaller or (not so usual) a larger one. As long as the fish remains stable, it should be possible to catch it eventually.

The 'Induced Take'

Sometimes a fish remains interested in all your flies, but you find yourself becoming more and more agitated as it continues to refuse each offering. One answer that is often effective is to tease the fish by trying the 'induced take'. In this, you take the fly away from the fish at a point close enough that it can seize it if its feeding instinct is aroused.

In the same way as before, you cast the fly and allow it to drift towards the fish until it is a short distance in front of it. You then lift the rod smoothly so that the fly begins an ascent towards the surface. If the fish does not react immediately and seize the fly, it will usually at least show more interest than before. And if it continues to feed, you should persevere. For any interest it shows in a fly will increase with each pass of the fly, in the belief, perhaps, that a hatch has started. It can be a very rewarding and satisfying experience to catch a fish after tempting it for twenty or thirty minutes with the same nymph.

Wise Fish

A feeding fish that is alarmed by the entry of an artificial fly into the water is a sign of bad luck or bad fishing. A wise fish that has been in the water for some time and has been hooked on a particular pattern may bolt if it sees that pattern again. If it recognizes that a line splashing on the water was part of the hooking process, it will bolt also at the sight or sound of a fly-line. The remedy, therefore, is in the flyfisher's hands—be careful. An alarmed fish that is nymphing will return to the same feeding station or close by within a short time if undisturbed, so it is worth resting it.

The Black-and-Peacock Spider is a fly that will catch a fish under most conditions. The original tying was meant to represent a water-snail, but since it was first tied by Tom Ivens, many variations have been introduced. These include varying the colour of the body or the hackle, or both. It can be fished on a sinking or a floating line, and is best fished slowly.

Still-Water Fishing

Fishing for sea trout on a Scottish loch, but with the boat drifting broadside as in the traditional style.

Look at any stretch of so-called 'still water', and you will appreciate fairly rapidly that the water is never actually still. There is always a current created by the wind, or a movement due to temperature changes. The effect of the wind is very important, because it usually has a bearing on where the fish are feeding. Weedy areas also attract fish for various reasons, such as shade, camouflage, and the presence of food.

The chief difference between still-water fishing and river fishing in that in still waters the fish have to travel to find their food. In running water, on the other hand, the food is carried to the fish by the current, and they simply move higher or lower in the water to intercept it.

Wind Effects on Water

Wind blowing across the surface of a lake or reservoir causes waves, which hit the leeward bank and rebound off it. If the wind is blowing head-on to the bank, the waves usually bounce back in the opposite direction. But if the wind is blowing at an angle to the bank, the waves will cause a current along the bank that sooner or later hits a corner and then comes away from the bank.

On the upwind (or windward) bank, the wind may be cooling the water or even warming it, and this will affect the fishing. As a rule, fish will stay in the warmest water so long as it contains plenty of oxygen. In very hot weather shallows do not contain much oxygen, but the wind does oxygenate the water to a certain extent.

Wind Effects on Fish

Where the wind blows into the bank, it stirs up the bottom, and the fish will be attracted by any food also stirred up in this way. The current created by the wind carries this food in the water, so you can reasonably expect to find fish in this current if they are feeding beneath the surface. Fish that are rising to surface food, however, may well reverse the pattern and rise on the upwind bank to insects that have been carried off the land.

For these reasons, it is usually a safe bet to begin fishing for fish feeding on land-bred insects on the upwind bank, and for predatory fish near weeds or deep water.

Choice of Fly

For fishing with the wind to the side, you should try a floating line in conjunction with a nymph or team of nymphs. A weighted fly, such as a Pheasant-Tail Nymph or a shrimp or corixa (water-beetle), could produce results in these conditions. Cast across the wind, and retrieve the fly very slowly after it has sunk sufficiently. Alternatively, you can leave it to swing round, the line being

dragged in a bow with the wind, and not retrieve it until it drifts into the bank.

If this method is showing no signs of bearing fruit, try fishing the fly either higher in the water or deeper, depending on where you made your first efforts. Once you make contact with a fish, continue fishing at that depth.

If the fly you are using is not being accepted, try a different one fished in the same way. With fish that are feeding on the bottom, a shrimp is usually a good choice, because in most still waters there is an abundance of them, and they are popular with all species of fish.

You may find that the fish are following a kind of migratory pattern, moving up the wind and feeding on food carried down on the way (they will be reasonably high in the water), and then returning down the wind at a much deeper level, even on the bottom. And although they are usually travelling much faster on the bottom, they will feed there until they

Left: Bank fishing from a dam. If the fish do not come to you, move along the bank until you contact them. Cast from A, retrieve from B; cast from B, retrieve from C, etc.

Below left: Fishing from the point of a bank. Cast from position X. The wind will blow the line into a bow on a slow retrieve.

Right: Having worked out the correct method, an angler is rewarded with a fighting trout.

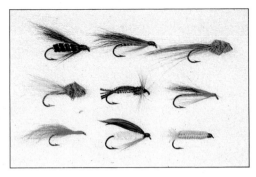

A selection of reservoir flies—all the average angler would need to fish a large still water. The majority of them are tied to represent fry or other items of food. The others are simply attractors, which should be fished fast. They are all effective on their day.

reach the leeward bank. Then they repeat the process. The best way to tempt these 'migratory' fish is with a team of nymphs or small wet flies on a floating line. Fish them across the wind and from a protruding point of land if possible. As a rule, the depth at which you fish the flies is crucial.

Whether fishing across the wind in this way or into a light wind, you will be covering the feeding fish. If none are being caught, it is simply a question of intelligent trial and error, varying the colour or size of the flies,

fishing deeper or not so deep, and varying the speed of retrieve.

Greasing the Leader

It is necessary to grease the leader when the fish are feeding very close to the surface (you will see them humping). Grease it to within a short distance of the flies, to ensure that they fish high in the water. Greasing the leader, however, does produce the problem of line wake. The wake occurs because, as the flies are being retrieved, the floating line and leader, and especially any dropper knots,

disturb the water surface. The faster the retrieve, the more disturbance there is. On windy days, this is not so serious. But on calm or fairly calm days it can be unforgiving, and in order to minimize line wake care must be taken to keep the retrieve smooth and even.

Sinking the Leader
If the fish are occasionally showing but not really rising steadily, it may be that they are still feeding in the same way, but deeper. In this event, the leader should be treated to make it sink. And if it needs to fish deeper than a normal sinking rate will allow, again you should use a weighted fly somewhere on the cast.

Using a Sinking Line
It may be possible to fish the water with a sinking line. It is quite acceptable, and sometimes a very good idea, to use a sinking line with a team of flies or to use a small lure in an effort to take fish that may otherwise prove difficult. Apart from being able to fish a fly at exactly the chosen depth, the main advantage of a sinking line is that there is no line wake, and a very slow-sinking line will enable you to fish at the same depth as a floating line.

You will also need a sinking line for predatory fish, because they are usually to be found in deep water or weedy stretches, near the bed of the reservoir or lake. They occasionally move from their lie to find food, and then return to the same area to digest it. As a rule, the chances of catching a big fish on a lure are better than on

nymph (gratifyingly, though, this is not always so). In weedy areas, where the water is usually shallower, a slow-sinking line is preferable. But in deeper water, it would take too long to reach the bottom, and a fast-sinking line will buy you more actual fishing time.

When retrieving a sinking line, you should hold the rod tip low so that the rod points down the line. Watch the line between the rod and the water for movement, because you might not feel a take at the rod until too late. As a rule, the takes are quite positive and the fish will pull hard or even 'smash' at the fly. But in any event, you should not make your strike until you feel the fish pulling at the fly hard and long. All you need to do is lift the rod positively, and the fish should be hooked. To snatch the rod in a strike could take the lure out of its mouth.

A flyfisher displays a trout safely in the net. The next step is to deliver the priest.

Water Temperature

Temperature has a marked effect on fish. They are more inclined to chase a fly in warmer water. The fly should be fished to give it the best chance of arousing the fishes' feeding instincts. In cooler water, therefore, a slow retrieve is best, so that the fly appears to be an easy meal. In warmer water, on the other hand, the fly should appear to be trying to escape, and a faster retrieve will probably be more successful. Nevertheless, all speeds of retrieve should be tried until you find the right one.

Boat Fishing

A boat is simply a means of taking the flyfisher to the fish. In certain circumstances you will anchor the boat, in others you will fish from a drifting boat.

Boat fishing should be practised

Wake flies, as their name implies, are fished on the surface to create a wake, which attracts fish to them. They are most successful in dull conditions.

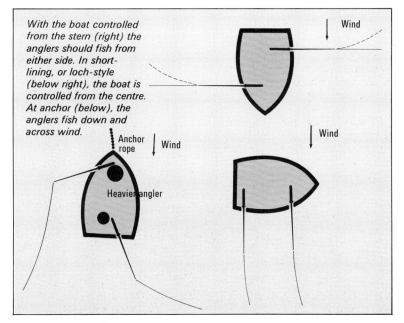

With the boat controlled from the stern (right) the anglers should fish from either side. In short-lining, or loch-style (below right), the boat is controlled from the centre. At anchor (below), the anglers fish down and across wind.

Wind

Anchor rope | Wind

Heavier angler

Wind

These anglers demonstrate perfectly why wading can be detrimental to flyfishing! They are not really casting a great deal farther as a result; there is no bank weed to overcome; and they are forming a 'picket line' that will prevent shy fish from coming close to the shore-line.

with considerable intelligent forethought. To begin with, the equipment in the boat should be so arranged that a person fishing at each end has a clear space in which to allow retrieved line to fall. Blundering about in the boat causes vibrations in the water and alarms the fish, so everything required should be placed ready to hand. For example, the landing net should be accessible from either end, and each angler's tackle should be at a separate end of the boat. This should include lunch as well as flies.

Two flyfishers in a boat is usually the optimum number, unless the boat is very large or if there will be no false casting. It is unwise to crowd a boat, and accidents can easily occur if too many fly-lines are being used in too restricted a space. To fish two rods on the same side of the boat would be a waste of valuable water, so the two should cast from opposite sides unless a strong wind makes it impossible.

If the fish appear to be concentrated in a particular area, you should use an anchor. Secure it to the bow of the boat and drop it to maintain the boat within casting distance of the fish (but *not* among the fish). In this way it is possible to fish into the leeward shore. Drifting in a boat along a shore can produce dramatic results. Silence is important when fishing from a boat, especially one at anchor.

Trolling

Sometimes fish can be very wary, particularly later in the season, and they learn to connect a lure retrieved in a stop-go motion with danger. Trolling is really a last resort, a method reserved for deep waters and days when all else has failed. But it may produce a big fish.

In trolling, a sinking line is cast out and trailed behind the boat. As a rule, the longer the line being trailed, the deeper the fly fishes. The rod should be held flat and point towards the rear of the boat.

The idea is to row about until you make contact with a fish. There is no retrieve, and the speed of the fly depends on the speed of the boat. Changing direction means that the fly is not always directly behind the boat, and it also varies the speed of the fly.

Tandem lures provide a larger target for the fish.

74

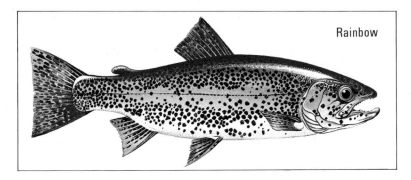

Rainbow

Trout

Of the game fish regularly sought on fly, the trout is the most numerous, the most accessible, and the easiest to rear artificially. And because trout fishing is so readily available, the trout has become a popular fish worldwide.

But most trout anglers will agree that the foremost reason for flyfishing

Tiger trout are a new experimental form of hybrid which are being stocked in a few waters and are becoming renowned for their fighting ability. This one is nearing the end of its fight and is being drawn toward the net. The bright fly can be seen in the side of its mouth.

for trout is that it is such a hard-fighting fish. A trout in good condition hooked on fly tackle will give a tremendous fight from the split second that the hook is driven home.

The trout also populates some lovely rivers in scenic countryside. Feeling part of nature in such areas adds to the enjoyment of the fishing.

There are times when trout appear to be the simplest of fishes, taking almost any fly that is cast within reasonable distance of them. Yet at other times they will avidly feed within plain sight and refuse all sizes, patterns, and colours. When that happens, though, it should make you fish even harder rather than discourage. And whatever type of day you have, a full day's trout fishing will drain every ounce of your energy.

Trout Fishing Round the World

The trout, in its various forms, populates rivers and lakes in most temperate parts of the world. To a large degree, this is due to the influence of man, who has introduced certain species to places where they had not previously existed.

Rainbow and brown trout are fished for throughout the world, and brook trout have achieved widespread popularity in recent years. There are also the local varieties, which are pursued with just as much enthusiasm, such as the cutthroat and the Dolly Varden of North America. And then there are the cross-bred varieties, such as cheetah, zebra, and tiger trout. These are bred by using the eggs of one species and fertilizing them with the milt from another. The result is a 'mule', which may have the qualities of both parent fish, but which is infertile.

Most regions of the world have rivers or lakes that offer exceptional trout fishing, and among the most well known are the chalk streams of England, the rapid rivers and limestone streams of North America, the

Above: A secluded mountain lake in Australia.

Left: A cultivated small fishery in Hampshire, England, Avington is famous for its world-record rainbows.

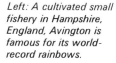

Right: Fishing the Falls Pool, in Perth, Scotland.

Below: Fishing a North American water from a natural dam, constructed by beavers.

the human population is low, the country wild and rugged, and the waters vast and deep. These fish present a great challenge to all flyfishers because of their habitat and restricted feeding habits, which make them difficult to tempt on fly, and, most of all, because of their bulk.

In the wild and long rivers of relatively unspoiled and unpolluted regions, as found in South America and New Zealand, the trout, both brown and rainbow, will also grow to exceptional proportions. And with this great bulk and their speed through the water, they provide a real test of skill for any angler.

But a trout does not have to be large to be a challenge. Some of the most enjoyable flyfishing can be for 'pan-sized' brown trout in moorland and mountain regions in almost any place where they can be found. The trout, in effect, is a bond between flyfishers from all parts of the world. Anglers travel from their own countries, even leaving behind exceptional trout fishing, to sample the sport in foreign waters. It is always a challenge to pit your wits against nature in a new environment, where the fish is unfamiliar and the unexpected can be relied upon.

slow, wide rivers of South America, the mountain lakes and snow-plain creeks of Australia, the lakes and swift rivers of New Zealand, and the loughs of Ireland.

Some regions encompass widely contrasting fishing. They offer trout of magnificent proportions that will take a fly readily and take all the line off the angler's reel before breaking free or stopping. While in the smaller waters of these places, the fish may be so timid that they have to be approached with the utmost caution and cast to with great accuracy and a first-class fly imitation.

The largest trout usually live in the largest lakes and rivers. Huge lake trout populate areas of North America and the British Isles where

Feeding Habits

Trout feed mainly on insects that are part of their natural habitat and other tiny items of food, such as small fry and crustaceans. But when they reach a size that is difficult to maintain, they become cannibals, avidly feeding on other species of fish and even on their own species in order to take in sufficient food.

The more a fish has to swim to find its food, the more food it will need to replenish its lost energy. The larger the fish, the more food it needs. Thus the larger fish tend to live in areas where food is readily available and they do not have to move far to find it. This applies particularly to brown trout. Rainbow trout tend to move about more anyway.

At most times of the year, trout will rise to the surface to take food. During warmer parts of the year, all trout will readily take floating or hatching insects, which are plentiful. An occasion when many fish are feeding on the surface is collectively known as a *rise*. Rises generally occur in the early hours, soon after dawn, or in late evening. You may see a rise during the day in dull, cloudy weather, but trout do not usually rise to the surface in bright sunlight.

Even when there is a rise, there are always fish feeding on the bottom on nymphs and on snails or shrimps.

Left: A natural blue-winged olive spinner (male). The olives in their various forms provide the food to induce trout to rise to nymphs or dry fly in still waters and streams. They are a welcome sight to all flyfishers because they are relatively easy to imitate.

Above: Spent mayflies on the water.
Left: A trout lazily intercepts a fly on a stream. It should be given plenty of time before striking if it takes an artificial like this.

It is every flyfisher's dream to witness substantial rainbows such as these in one pool. This mouth-watering photograph was taken in New Zealand at the appropriately named Paradise Valley.

Movements

In running water trout tend to take up a station—their lie. In this way, the running water brings food to them and they do not have to expend energy in swimming to find it—only in maintaining their position in the current.

In still water the trout must either move around to find its food or live in an area where the food will swim or drift by. A big trout needs a lot of large food items, and if the food supply at its lie is insufficient, it must rove the water to find more. In other words, you will find the fish where the food is.

It is also worth remembering that trout are inclined to move more in warmer water. In typical warm water with a plentiful hatch of fly life, the trout will swim up the wind, taking the insects as they are pushed along by the wind. The best way to fish for them in these circumstances is to cast across the wind with a floating line and a team of wet flies and nymphs (see page 62).

During long spells of hot and bright weather, trout tend to stay deep during the day. They will probably feed near the leeward bank, where the water is perhaps slightly more oxygenated by the wind movement. If there is no wind, they will feed only at odd times during the day for short intervals. In such conditions, the only way to catch fish is to fish deep all day long and hope to be in the right place.

During cooler weather, there is usually plenty of wind movement. The fish will almost invariably be at the leeward bank feeding on wind-blown food and food that has been stirred up by the water movement.

Four fine rainbow trout arranged in a pose for a photograph album. Although the line is an unnecessary embellishment, the rod, reel, and fly boxes each serve as a comparison with the actual size of the fish for future reference. It is surprising how such photographs will help you to recall a particular day's fishing or a favourite fly.

Trout Tackle

The choice of line depends on conditions and, as discussed in earlier chapters, is made by taking into consideration factors such as depth of water, rising fish, and so on. The real choice to be made in trout fishing lies with the rod.

Choice of rod is influenced to a great degree by personal preference, but common sense must also prevail. For instance, a short brook rod is ideal for fishing narrow streams, but would be hopeless for casting maximum distances on a large reservoir, casting a heavy line, or playing very large fish.

So to some extent your choice of rod is governed by the line to be used and then the type of water to be fished. If it is possible to use a light line and you will not be casting long distances, a medium-length rod is a pleasure to fish with. Coupled, say, with an AFTM 6 or 7 floating line, it would not be in the least tiring. But when fishing in an adverse wind, such as one blowing onto your casting arm or straight at you, a heavier line achieves more distance and you will find that a carbon-fibre rod, being

lighter, is easier to use. An exception is that when the wind is blowing onto your casting arm, you may find that some carbon-fibre rods are not stiff enough to keep the line away from your ear. In such conditions, glass-fibre rods will prove better and safer.

For boat fishing, where you are very close to the water surface, a long rod is preferable, because it keeps the line farther from the surface when casting. It is also easier to handle and easier to play fish with. Another item to bear in mind when boat fishing is the landing net. For wading or bank fishing, a folding landing net is more practicable, but for boat fishing the landing net should have a long, stout handle. Otherwise, sooner or later you will encounter a fish that sees the net and promptly dives under the boat—with the result that you lose it.

A *priest* is a short-handled implement with a weighted end, used to 'deliver the last rites' to a fish. It is essential to be able to dispatch the fish the instant it is landed (if it is to be kept), and priests range from plain metal to fancy stag horns. You will also need a pair of forceps or long-nosed pliers for removing difficult hooks without damaging the fly dressing.

Trout Flies

Trout have the infuriating and regular habit of becoming preoccupied with feeding on flies that are impossible to imitate, such as caenis or midges, because they are so small. At these times, although they will feed hard, they will often not be tempted by anything other than a natural insect. And as it is not possible (except with dapping) to use natural insects, such periods often produce only the odd fish or no fish at all.

But there are, of course, many times when the fish are preoccupied on an insect that is possible to imitate. Trout often rise to insects that hatch in the water, such as sedges, stoneflies, and mayflies. They will also steadily rise to a plentiful supply of terrestrial insects that have been blown onto the water, such as drone flies and crane flies (daddy-

The cranefly season begins as the weather cools towards autumn, and the natural insect (above) on the water can induce some large fish to feed on the surface. Natural insects may be dapped on the water or an artificial (as shown below) may be fished static or dapped. There are many variations on the type of artificials.

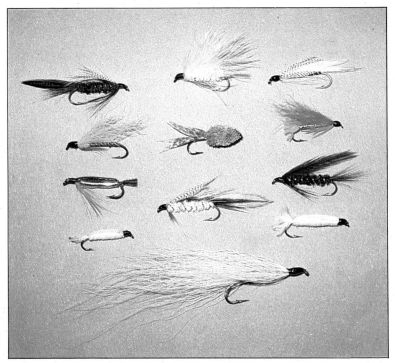

This selection of lures would serve the average trout fisher for a whole season.

long-legs), and have been known happily to mop up swarms of ants or bees from the surface.

When trout are preoccupied, you must first find out just what it is they are feeding on. In order to give the flyfisher a reasonable chance of tempting the trout whatever the prevailing conditions, a vast array of flies has been developed over the years, and all have their local or personal variations. The main point to remember is that they fall into three categories—imitators, attractors (sometimes called 'flashers'), and lures.

Imitators

These are tied as dry and wet flies and nymphs, and are intended to resemble the natural food on which the trout are feeding. You need not be overconcerned with precise details when using imitators, unless the trout are proving to be very difficult indeed. In many instances the trout will take a fly of the right size or silhouette, even though it may be the wrong colour. And sometimes they will take a fly for its colour when it is the wrong shape or size. Experience has no substitute, and fortune may also play a large part in determining whether a trout takes or not.

Attractors

These artificial flies could not possibly be an imitation of an insect because of their colour. They might, for instance, be the brilliant orange of the Whisky fly or the bright yellow and red of the Mickey Finn. Usually they are tied in the same style and shape as a wet fly and fished in the same way.

It is always a good idea to include an attractor fly on a leader with a team of flies—because if the imitators are not right, the attractor might tempt the fish, and if the imitators are correct, the attractor might bring the trout to them in the first place.

The purpose of the attractor is to bring the fish to the fly by arousing its curiosity, and then perhaps the fish will take the fly out of sheer aggression. If the trout are proving difficult to catch, an attractor fly cast close to them and fished fairly fast may well cause them to take the fly, even though it resembles nothing in nature. Attractors should always be fished fairly fast, on either a floating or a sinking line. But they are usually most effective fished across the wind

This rainbow trout has been hooked firmly in the gristle, probably the safest place to hook any fish.

Brook

on a floating line or from a drifting boat (see the chapter on *Still-Water Fishing*).

Lures

These are flies tied on larger, long-shanked or tandem hooks, and are intended to lure the big fish that are feeding on fry. However, with natural progression, some lures have proved so effective that they are now recognized imitator or attractor patterns, are tied on very much smaller hooks, and may be fished in the same way as a wet fly. In this way, they catch much smaller fish than was originally intended.

It is unusual to fish lures on a floating line, but this can prove effective. For instance, a Muddler Minnow fished through waves on a dull day with a floating line causes a wake and can be a deadly and most exciting exercise.

In the main, though, lures are fished on sinking lines and at a depth sensible enough to catch fish. In a water with deep-lying large fish, you would use a fast-sinking line and a large lure, such as a size 6 or 8 long-shank or larger. White and black appear to be the best colours.

As a rule of thumb, it is best to fish lures slowly. Sometimes the takes can be very hard, but they usually appear as slow as if the fly had been caught on weed. You should not strike hard at these pulls until they materialize as a fish definitely taking hold. In other words, do not pull at the trout until it is pulling at you. Lures tend to be most effective at the times of the day when fish are not rising to naturals, and in early and late season.

There are many types of boxes available to the flyfisher for the storage of flies, but the wooden folding type (right) tends to be most popular, even if it is not always the most convenient for carrying. The selection of artificial flies and lures shown in this box would cater for most anglers on most waters.

Brown

Specimen Trout

Many anglers flyfish for trout for a very long time without ever taking one of eye-opening proportions—although every fish has something to recommend it, and most anglers enjoy every fish they catch. But fortune does play a large part in our fishing, because it is not normally possible to choose which fish takes our fly in a vast water. So, as a rule, it is the small fish, being more numerous, that get to the fly first. It is only by putting in as many hours

This 'jumbo' rainbow trout is a specimen from Avington, Hampshire.

as possible into your fishing that you will increase your share of luck.

The alternative to fishing long and often is to attend one of the many waters that now stock plenty of huge rainbow trout in a relatively small space. In this way your chances of taking a specimen trout are immediately increased. But to assume that these large fish, which may be seen cruising the margins and sometimes feeding hard, are queueing up to take your fly is bound to lead to disappointment.

You must remember that clear water is always a lot deeper than it appears to be, and so your fly will need a long time to sink. The tackle required is relative to the length of leader you are using, but a medium-length rod, if possible, is a good choice. In running water, you should fish in the same way as either dry-fly or nymph-fishing, according to whether or not the fish is rising. But the tactics are different in still water, because you have to intercept the fish.

It may happen that the large trout you are stalking has seen it all before, and as soon as your rod is waved in readiness for the cast it bolts. The only consolation is that it will

A brown trout being correctly netted. It has been played out and has allowed itself to be drawn over the net on its side and with its head up. In less than another second, the net will be lifted and the fish will be engulfed. The tension can then be released on the rod and all energy diverted to lifting the fish from the water.

probably at some time reappear and offer you another opportunity. The essential thing is to get the fly down to the fish as quickly as possible, and this will probably mean using a leaded nymph. It might well be necessary for you to cast the fly to the bottom and leave it there to await the trout's return. Once you have pre-sented your fly, it is then up to the trout. The only help you can give it is movement, by drawing the fly away from the fish. This, the so-called 'induced take' (described on page 68), is an extremely important tactic in flyfishing for trout whatever method you are using and whatever the size of your quarry.

Stocking a water with trout fresh from the hatchery. As the demand on natural stocks of trout increase, it is necessary to subsidise them with artificially reared trout. In this picture, trout are being released by hand into a stream. Much larger amounts may be delivered by lorries into large still waters or large rivers. Whichever way they are released, they must be tended to carefully and be provided with oxygen on their journey to the water.

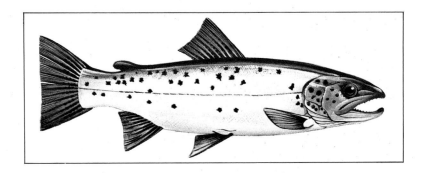

Sea Trout

The sea trout is enthusiastically pursued largely for the great sport it offers. But it also possesses, for most anglers, a kind of mystique, because of its wild nature and its habitat.

In recent times, the theory has been pushed that sea trout fishing is worthwhile only during the hours of darkness. While it cannot be denied that the fishing is better at night, it is by no means true that fishing for sea trout in daylight is a futile pursuit. It is better if there is some colour to the water, as these fish are extremely wary

and shy of tackle that is too obvious or being awkwardly fished. In clear water, even at night, the tackle must be scaled down, and small flies used in preference to large ones, which would be acceptable in coloured water.

Sea trout have almost exactly the same life-cycle as salmon. They are born in fresh water, migrate to the sea, and return to spawn. They tend to be more numerous than salmon, and there are usually sea trout in rivers connected to the sea at all

Both of these sea-trout flies are a variation of the Teal Blue and Silver. The tube fly is tied with a hair wing, as is usually the case with such flies, and the wing of the traditionally dressed fly consists of sections from the barred feather of a teal duck. Either fly is very effective for sea trout, and the sizes can be varied to suit conditions.

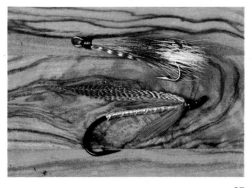

A beautifully proportioned sea trout taken on fly (above) and two smaller sea trout, also taken on fly (right). Depending on the water and the time of year of its capture, a sea trout of any size is a fish of merit, and anglers from all over the world brave the worst conditions in the attempt to catch them.

times of the year. Where a large still water is connected to the sea, they will travel into it, to spawn in any small feeder streams, and live for a time as trout, even feeding in the same way.

The best time to fish for sea trout in the rivers during daylight is when there has been a spate and the water is dropping back to a more normal level. The fish will be running steadily then, and are more easily tempted. But when the water is in full flood, they travel quickly and tend to ignore

all flies offered. And anyway, when the water is high, flyfishing is always difficult.

Fishing Methods

The method of fishing for sea trout is more or less the same as that for salmon fishing (see pages 102–3), but the tackle need not be so heavy. A single-handed rod is usually sufficient, with either a floating or a sinking line, depending on water conditions. The line is cast across the current and allowed to swing right round. The

Night Fishing for Sea Trout

The main advantages of fishing for sea trout at night are that the fish are more willing then to accept a fly and their keen sight and awareness are more easily overcome. There is also the fact that night fishing has a certain magic about it that appeals to the hunting instincts of most anglers.

The best conditions are fairly low water and warm, settled weather. The method of fishing is the same as for during the day, but certain precautions must be taken to lessen the chances of accidents.

During the day, reconnoitre the water to be fished, noting the likely holding spots (lies) and, especially, the possible snags. If you intend to wade, you should test the bottom by wading into the water and noting the position of any deep holes or any places where you might trip. If the casting is limited by obstructions, you should make a note of distances and directions in which your back or forward cast must go to avoid them. Having satisfied yourself that you know the water inside-out, you will be ready to start after darkness has fallen.

Never attempt to fish anywhere that you have not established as perfectly safe. Avoid heavy line splash. On a cloudless, moonlit night with no wind, you will find that the fish tend to get 'spooked' very easily.

A lady angler, undaunted by adverse weather conditions, brings a sea trout to the net in a Hebridean loch. The netting is being carried out by a ghillie. Notice the wide beam of the boat for extra stability. The oars are in the water because the ghillie has been manoeuvring the boat.

take may be just a gentle pluck, but is often fairly violent and the ensuing fight filled with savage leaps and rod-bending runs across and down the current. It is generally easier to land sea trout than salmon because of their more modest size, and a fairly large landing net should be ample equipment.

The types of river inhabited by sea trout are the same as for salmon and their lies are similar. Look for them in quiet stretches of water leading into rapid runs or at the top of the runs. The fish tend to rest either before attempting to overcome the obstacles or after expending their energy in overcoming them.

Fishing for sea trout in inland lakes, on the other hand, is very similar to the traditional style of trout fishing. The boat is allowed to drift freely, broadside to the wind, with an angler at each end and perhaps a boatman to stabilize it with oars. Each angler casts a short line down the wind with a team of flies. The team is retrieved to the boat, and the process is repeated until the end of the drift is reached. The boat is then returned up the wind to the head of the drift, and fishing is continued. If the first drift is unsuccessful, a fresh area should be tried.

At times, only very small sea trout will be encountered. But with the right tackle, you will find they give an equally good account of themselves as their larger bretheren on heavier

Two excellent medium-sized sea trout from Loch Voshimid, in the Outer Hebrides of Scotland. The lower and larger fish appears to have been in freshwater longer, because it is slightly darker than the smaller one. Sea trout are silver when fresh in from the sea, and the longer they are in freshwater the darker they become.

tackle, and provide spectacular sport and perhaps more of it.

Choice of Fly

There is a large amount of speculation as to whether sea trout feed in freshwater or not. It is reasonably certain, however, that they do feed after they have been in freshwater for a while, and some feed in the estuary. And they can be caught on flies that most fish. This situation is thoroughly confusing for a newcomer to sea trout, and the only answer really is to rely to a large degree on local knowledge of the water, and try to seek this before actually fishing.

The most popular sea trout fly is probably the Teal-Blue and Silver, and recently a Welsh pattern known as the Dai Ben has proved to be a good fly. Basically, the chief require-

probably represent food to them because of the absence of colour or flash. But as the sea trout is a particularly aggressive fish, it is probably best to try a fly with some attractive qualities by way of flash or colour at some stage of your fishing expedition.

As with all types of flyfishing, one angler finds that a particular fly fishes well for him, while another will prefer a different pattern. This is particularly true for sea trout fishing, and various fly patterns are advocated by experts as the ones that will catch

Sea trout flies can be of almost any size, depending on conditions. They are usually intended to attract the fish, but are not necessarily brightly coloured.

ment of a successful sea trout fly is its ability to be seen by the fish. In reasonably clear water this means a dark fly. A small one will work as well as one with colour. For fishing in the dark, a dark fly or one with plenty of flash is required. And at night it is generally advisable to use a larger fly than in daytime.

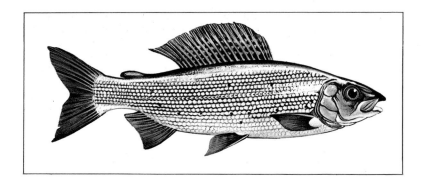

Grayling

The grayling inhabits the same type of water as the trout. By comparison with the trout, it has larger scales, is slimier and stronger smelling, and does not fight as hard at the times of the year when it is breeding. At these times, it becomes an ugly, dark fish in contrast to its otherwise healthy silvery appearance.

But when the grayling is in a fighting mood, it is quite a dashing fish, using its graceful large dorsal fin to very good effect in a swift current.

The main crime of the grayling in the eyes of trout-farmers and water-owners is that it is said to compete with trout for food. And as it breeds much more freely than trout in stocked waters, a stream can easily become overrun by small grayling.

Left: Nymphs with seals-fur bodies and lead under the dressing (to take them to the bottom). These are favourite flies for grayling if they are not inclined to rise or are resting at the bottom of a deep pool or run.

While it is true that grayling eat the same food as trout, this has been no justification for the indiscriminate culling of the fish that has taken place. As a result, there are now no grayling present in some waters where they used to thrive. They have much to offer the flyfisher, and careful control of the fish could result in an enjoyable mixed fishery.

On days when trout are reluctant to rise to the fly, you will always find sufficient grayling to fish for. In general, they are not as discerning as trout, and once feeding they tend to carry on, and will not become pre-occupied as trout do. Once hooked, they will fight as well as any member of the salmon family up to the time they are netted.

The grayling rise tends to be more of a slash at the fly than the sipping or sucking type of rise typical of the trout. This is probably because its mouth is situated very much on the underneath of its body, in the same way as bottom-feeding fish. The grayling will rise on the coldest of days—not as frequently as on warmer days, of course, but it can nevertheless provide sport in autumn and winter to cheer an otherwise dull day.

Flies and Fishing

If grayling are found to be rising, it is best to start with a small fly, either grey or black in colour. Fish it in the same way as dry flyfishing for trout, and with just as much, if not more, caution, because grayling tend to shoal more and if you scare one you scare them all. When the fish takes the fly, it can be struck slightly earlier than the trout because of the angle of its mouth. Sometimes, a dry fly that 'drags' slightly will be taken

An operation for the netting of grayling on a trout river so that they may be removed in order to lessen the competition for food. The grayling once netted will not necessarily be destroyed. Hopefully, they will be transported to new waters where they are welcome to provide sport for other anglers. In more recent years, the grayling does seem to have become more plentiful in Britain owing to growing support from anglers who deplore the Victorian habit of killing all fish in a trout stream. Including the trout when caught, small fish of non-predatory species are usually worth returning alive.

Above: An angler plays a grayling on the River Test in Hampshire. The surroundings are typically idyllic.

Left: With its adorning dorsal fin and its graceful shape and colouring, it is easy to see why the grayling is sometimes known as 'the lady of the stream'.

when a conventionally fished one is refused.

If you can see grayling feeding on the bottom of the stream, fish for them in the same way as you would fish an upstream nymph for trout, using a weighted fly that will trundle along the bottom to the fish. Good flies to try in such circumstances are leaded shrimps and weighted Pheasant-Tail Nymphs.

Grayling seem to be particularly susceptible to the induced take. Once they have fixed their eye on the fly and it is taken away from them, they will often move forward with a flick of

their tail and take the fly as it rises in the water. Again, this type of fishing can be lots of sport on otherwise slow days.

If grayling are known to be in a water, it is usually a fairly easy matter to find them. The bigger fish will be in the deep holes and slow eddies, and the more average fish will be in almost any part of the water—in the pools and also in the faster water. Nearly all grayling seem to favour wooded areas. But stalk them carefully. For if they see you, you will not be given the opportunity to cast for them.

Salmon

The salmon is often referred to as the 'king of fishes', and every angler who has ever grassed a bright fresh-run salmon after a battle filled with thrilling runs and magnificent leaps will agree with that description.

Apart from its fine appearance and superb fighting qualities, the salmon also offers excellent eating and is one of the most expensive items on many menus. For this reason, it has been unmercifully exploited and is not nearly as numerous now as it was before World War II. This commercial exploitation is made easy because the salmon spends the greater part of its life at sea, returning to freshwater to spawn in the river in which it was born. In addition to indiscriminate netting in the estuaries, some of the feeding grounds at sea have been discovered, and this has resulted in netting on a massive scale despite efforts to control it.

Fortunately, some areas still have reasonable or good runs of salmon returning from the sea, and salmon fishing is still possible with sporting methods, though it has become very expensive in the better areas. Fly-fishing for salmon can be very frustrating at times, because water conditions are critical—the water must not be too coloured or too high or low. And although catching a salmon on fly is the most rewarding of experiences, the art is not as widely practised throughout the world as spinning or bait fishing.

A salmon displays grace and power as it leaps clear of the water.

Left: A Pacific salmon, the coho.

Right: The rollcast is popular when salmon-fishing in restricted spaces. The drag of the water is used to work the rod, as clearly demonstrated in the photograph.
Below right: Although this catch of salmon was probably not all taken on fly, it is the sort of catch that many flyfishers dream of. It was taken from the River Vosso, in Norway, in a single day. Sadly, very few rivers are now capable of yielding such a magnificent capture of Atlantic salmon.

Salmon Fishing Around the World

The salmon is almost exclusive to the Northern Hemisphere. The Atlantic salmon is a single species, but the Pacific salmon, found naturally in North America but transplanted successfully to New Zealand, is subdivided into several species, including the Coho, Chinook, and Sockeye.

The Atlantic salmon is the one sought mainly by flyfishing methods. It is found in North America, but is more popular in northern Europe—the British Isles, Norway, Sweden, Greenland, and Iceland—where it is considered to be the ultimate quarry. Anglers travel the world to visit these places for the salmon fishing.

The main requirement for salmon is that they have absolutely pure, pollution-free water in which to run and spawn. This ensures that they occupy some of the most beautiful and wild countryside in the world,

which adds to the attraction of fishing for them.

Pacific salmon are generally not as highly regarded for their sporting qualities, even though some grow to a larger size than their Atlantic counterparts. And neither are they as highly prized at the table.

The ultimate in salmon, sought after only by the few anglers with the necessary time and wealth, is the huchen. This large salmon lives chiefly in the cooler rivers of the USSR and the Danube system. It does not migrate to the sea, and demands such pure water for its habitat that it has become quite rare. The main reason for its reputation is that it is a particularly wild fish, with monumental strength and stamina, and will fight with savage power from the moment it is hooked until it is grassed.

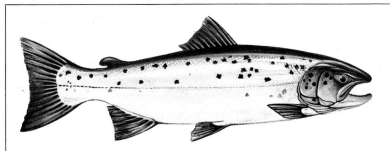

Life Cycle of the Salmon

It is a well known fact that the salmon is born in the river, migrates to the sea, and then returns to the river of its birth to spawn, fighting its way over seemingly impossible obstacles to reach its objective. Having done so, it returns to the sea until the next year.

It is thought that salmon cannot feed in freshwater because their stomach atrophies soon after entry into the river. So no really concrete reason as to why they take flies—or prawns or worms—can be put forward, although they will take worms, and sometimes other baits, well into their throats.

After spawning, the hen salmon buries the fertilized eggs in a river-bed nest of scooped gravel known as a *redd*. It then tries to return as a kelt to sea, leaving the eggs to hatch. The salmon fry grows into a salmon *parr*, and when it is old enough and strong enough to make the journey, having remained in the river usually for between one and three years, it too travels downstream (now silvery and called a *smolt*) and out to sea. After a year at sea, some salmon return for their first spawning as *grilse*, usually

in the spring. Having spawned, they return to the sea, and so the cycle continues.

There are usually two major runs of salmon each year, one in spring and one in autumn. The spring-run fish are usually smaller. They may even stay in the river until the autumn and spawn and then return with the bigger fish. A salmon fresh in from the sea is bright and clean, possibly with sea lice attached. One that has been in the river for a while turns dark.

There are two types of salmon that are undesirable to the angler—the kelt and the baggot. A *kelt* is a fish that has spawned and is on its return journey, a spent fish that will be thin and dark—it should be carefully returned. A *baggot* is a kind of rogue salmon that has stayed in the river a long time—it too, should be returned.

Every spring and autumn, salmon leave the sea (1) to begin their remarkable journey back to their spawning grounds, braving rapids and falls as they fight their way upstream (2). At the breeding grounds they lay their eggs on the river bed (3). Tiny salmon hatch from the eggs (4), and when they are strong enough, after 1–3 years, they 'return' to the sea as smolts (5).

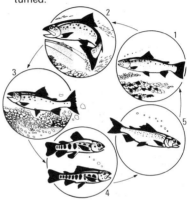

Left: The ghillie watches patiently with net and tailer in hand, while the angler seeks his quarry.

Salmon Tackle

Being heavier and far stronger than the other game fish, the salmon calls for rods with great strength and reels that hold a large amount of line. Carbon-fibre rods up to 20 ft (6m) long are available, and, despite the lightness of the material compared with cane rods of equivalent length, are still designed to be used two-handed. The reel should be large enough to hold a sufficient length of backing line in addition to the fly-line.

In order to fish more water and follow the fish if it is too strong to be held within a reasonable distance, special waders are often used for salmon fishing. These are called chest-waders and, as the name implies, are waders with additional waterproof material to bring them up to the chest.

Special equipment is also generally needed for landing the catch. There are a number of options, depending on the type of water being fished. The *gaff*, a metal hook on a pole, is slipped over the fish's back and the hook sunk into the fish. The *tailer*, a spring-loaded metal noose on a handle, is used to secure the fish by its tail. Or an outsize landing net may be used in the same way as for other fish.

Salmon Flies

Originally, salmon flies were tied on hooks with a small piece of doubled gut used as an eye, which was whipped to the shank. Nowadays, the more usual single salmon hook is up-eyed with a forged bend, and painted black.

Most salmon flies are gaudy affairs of many colours and of such intricate detail in the pattern that all the incorporated features make them lengthy and expensive flies to tie. Such patterns include the Jock Scott, Hairy Mary, Yellow Dog, and many more. Of the more recent flies, the Stoat's Tail, a plain, drab, dark fly, is now accounting for many fish, especially in low water in summer. Also popular now and widely used is the tube fly. This is not the name of a pattern, as tube flies can be dressed in many patterns, but the name of a style of dressing. Animal hair is the chief material used, and it is dressed around a plain tube, the length of which varies considerably. The line is then inserted through the tube and tied to a treble hook. As a result, the chances of the hook taking a firm hold on the fish are in theory increased.

Salmon hooks forged as doubles are also commonly used, and the dressing is tied direct to these.

A selection of salmon flies of new and traditional patterns. Like sea trout flies, they are meant mainly to attract the fish. But during low water, the flies used are usually small and dark.

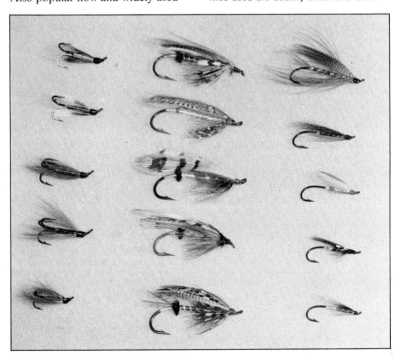

A very realistic imitation of a prawn tied with latex.

In the main, salmon flies are designed to irritate the fish into taking. The only really successful imitative flies are the numerous prawn and shrimp patterns, which obviously remind the fish of its sea life and will persuade it to take.

The size of hooks used varies greatly, from a number 10 upwards to a size 1. Generally, if the water is clear you should use a smaller pattern, and if the water is both low and clear a very small pattern such as a 10. These flies are so small that fancy dressing cannot be used, and so they are usually fairly plain.

The chief materials used for tying salmon flies are normal hackles with many different colours. Blues, reds, and yellows are commonplace. Wing fibres and hair are also regular constituents. Flies tied with hair may be plainer, because the hair moves in the water, giving life to the fly. With hackles, however, you may need all sorts of glitter and bristly effects. There is no doubt that the hackle-tied and feather flies look the prettiest, but they are not necessarily the best.

These tube flies show the variation in colour and size. The treble hook provides a 360° hooking ability, and the absence of a long shank leaves the fish with no leverage to help it loosen the hook.

Above: Mending line upstream to stop the fly skating over the surface. Below right: Casting on the River Dee in Scotland, a famous salmon river.

Fishing

The most important aspect of salmon-fishing technique is control of the line in the water. It governs the speed and depth of the flies. Salmon do not feed in fresh water, and the flies are more accurately called lures. On some waters it may be possible to tempt fish with a dry fly, but it is more usual to use a wet fly in conjunction with a floating line or sink-tip or fully sunken line.

The method of fishing for salmon is in many ways like downstream flyfishing for trout. But the salmon is a wild creature from the sea in a strange environment, and it is easily 'spooked'. For this reason, you do not cover a salmon time and time

again. You cover it once, and then rest it if it does not take.

On every salmon river you will find stretches of water that contain no fish. You will find the salmon in pools or holding spots where they are resting in their lies on their upstream journey, or are waiting for more water to enter the river before they continue. These holding spots are nearly always apparent.

Starting at the top (the upstream end) of the water, cast across and slightly downstream. If there is fast water between you and the far side, it may be necessary to mend your line by throwing a little more line than required upstream. This allows the fly to sink instead of skittering across the surface.

Fish the cast out until the line is hanging downstream. Then retrieve the line and, taking about two paces downstream, repeat the procedure. Do not fish from the same spot with the same fly again.

Never hold the line or strike as soon as you feel a take. The salmon will be rising from near the bottom to take your fly, and a strike made too early will certainly mean a lost fish and one that will not rise again. Simply hold the rod, allowing the yard or so loop of line between reel and butt ring to run out under slight tension of the forefinger, and the salmon will take the line as it returns to its lie. Then lift the rod firmly as the pull of the fish is felt.

If you know that a fish is in a pool or holding spot but has refused your fly, rest it and return later to try again with a different fly or perhaps a bigger fly. If, on the other hand, the salmon bulges at your fly, or it shows its apparent interest in some other way, but still refuses to take, it is probably because your fly is too big. Simply change the fly for one of the same pattern but a size smaller, and you should then take the fish. If not, rest it again and return later.

Wading into midstream in order to be able to fish the whole of the river efficiently.

When you think about it, hooking a salmon is quite an achievement, for it entails deceiving a wild creature into accepting an offering that it does not need. But having done so, it will now throw every ounce of its considerable strength into ridding itself of the restraining influence. Probably its first instinctive move will be to try to return to the sea, and your first consideration must be to maintain contact with it. You can usually do this better if you are on land, where you can follow your fish if need be. So if you are in the water, you should make for the bank carefully, if this is possible and would give you an advantage. By keeping a steady pressure on the fish and not allowing it to get too far from you, and providing the hook holds fast, you will eventually tire it. But be prepared at all times for it to turn about suddenly and run in the opposite direction. This could give it the slack it needs to shed the hook. If it 'sulks'—takes up a position at the bottom or perhaps behind a rock and refuses to budge— just maintain a steady pressure and it will probably move from its lie in time. At all times, if possible, keep the rod held high, as this will help the line clear underwater obstructions.

Landing the Catch

Having played out your salmon, the next step is to grass it. This can be done with the equipment described earlier, or with no aid at all, by *handtailing*.

The salmon is unique among fish in that it has a wrist to its tail before the tail fin starts. That is why it is possible to use a tailer. If you are wading, this is the best instrument to use. With the fish wallowing in front of you, simply place the sprung wire noose over its tail and release it. The noose will then tighten and hold the fish fast, enabling you to wade ashore with it.

A gaff is employed more usually with particularly heavy fish. The metal hook is sunk into the fish at about its point of balance so that it can then be heaved ashore. Gaffing should be done if possible from the bank. Many anglers, however, regard it as an abhorrent method and prefer a large landing net employed in the usual way.

Handtailing should be tried only on average-size fish or as a last resort on heavier fish. On gently sloping banks, if the salmon is drawn into the shallow water head first until it is on its side, its struggles will take it farther up the bank, where you can grasp it and carry it from the water. Salmon may also be handtailed from shallow water, although larger ones could become unmanageable.

Above: A salmon, having been played into shallow water, is hand-tailed ashore.

Right: A particularly fine Atlantic salmon from the River Vosso, in Norway. Although a salmon of this size could be hand-tailed, it is more usual to gaff suah a fish at its point of balance, when it can then be heaved ashore. Otherwise, its strength could help it break free if it has not been played out in the proper manner.

Coarse Fish

In most parts of the world, anglers are fortunate in that they can choose the fish they wish to catch on fly. But in some places only coarse fish are present. Not so long ago few fisher-

A specimen bream taken from a still water on a fly fished deep and slow. This species is not a predator, and the fly is fished in this way because of its bottom-feeding habits. Large shoals are usually found in weedy areas, and it should be possible to catch a great number once they have been located. A lure was used to capture this fish, which it probably mistook for a leech, but nymphs are also very effective.

men would have attempted to catch a coarse fish on fly, but with the ever-changing approach of anglers everywhere it is now becoming almost commonplace. And it is not only because of their availability that coarse fish are sought with the fly.

One advantage of coarse fish is that they are not expensive to fish for. This is generally because they are not as prized for their eating qualities and because they are more messy to handle than game fish. Nevertheless, they provide excellent sport, at times just as difficult to catch on fly, and they can be much larger than most game fish. In addition, some coarse fish, such as the North American bass, the zander, the perch, and the

pike, can be very tasty if taken from clean running water.

Many trout waters hold a large head of coarse fish, and the predators among them (pike especially) grow to outstanding proportions as a result of the ready-made supply of a high-protein trout diet. Not only are these predators regularly caught by accident, but some anglers fish for them as their principal quarry and treat the trout as secondary.

In the large still waters that support big trout, there will also be found large coarse fish besides the predators —fish such as rudd, bream, and roach. These can also provide good sport, because they will rise to dry flies and nymphs. The carp is another non-predator that will take a fly, and many of 10lb (4.5kg) or more have been caught. This is a double achievement—the hooking and the playing and landing on tackle that is really too light for the task.

In general, you will find that coarse fish are easier to tempt on the fly if they are feeding. They do tend to become more single-minded than the trout and other game fish, and only the predators will smash at a fly they do not want and which merely annoys or attracts them.

Unlike trout, most coarse fish tend to feed at one particular level, and only the predators will chase a fly. But like the game fish, they are also subject to water temperatures and are more prepared to move for a fly in warmer water than in cooler water.

Predators

Predatory coarse fish of one sort or another can be found in both still waters and running waters. You will usually find them where the water is

and appears lifelike in the water.

As for colour, you will probably find that a white fly will produce your best results. But for some fish a bright fly—red, yellow, blue, green, or even a combination of colours— will work best on certain days. In deep or coloured water, a bright yellow fly appears to be good for pike and zander, while perch react to a red fly.

Because you will be lure fishing, it is best to use a sinking line and fish the water at different depths until you find what level the fish are feeding at. Try fishing near areas that will provide cover for the fish as they lie in wait for their prey. Or look for concentrations of small fish, for this is usually a sign that predators are not far away.

Left: Trout waters such as this often hold a large head of coarse fish, and predators in particular grow big on their high-protein diet of trout.

Right: A superb pike taken from an English trout reservoir, where a high-protein diet of trout helped it reach this size.

slow-moving. In fast rivers where they are known to be present, look for the dead water or for very slow and deep areas.

If they have not been fished for before, they will take almost any type of lure that you like to cast to them. The best ones to use, however, are those with some movement, such as hairwing flies, and those with wings of marabou, which is vibrant

Non-Predators

Some fish that would normally be regarded as non-predators could perhaps also be classed as predators. The chub, for example, will rise beautifully to a dry fly one day and feed avidly on gudgeon or minnows the next. This is also true of others, but in the main those without teeth in their mouth will usually take a fly in the form of a nymph fished beneath the surface or

Above: A well marked perch, which was taken on fly from an English still water.

Above left: A typical fly used to take pike.

Left: A larger than average zander, or pike-perch. Both the perch and the zander feed almost exclusively on live or dead fish, and will take a fry-imitating lure worked close to the bottom or weed beds. Both fish when hooked will usually fight very well.

a dry fly fished on the surface. You use the same bàsic flyfishing techniques as you would for trout.

In still water, your coarse-fishing quarry—such as carp, bream, roach, or rudd—will generally be present on the bottom of the water, although roach and rudd rise avidly to surface flies on warm summer days. Whatever fly you use must be presented extremely slowly, and you will probably find a figure-of-eight retrieve best. For roach and bream, a white fly can sometimes produce very good results, and a small Baby Doll or White Chenille lure will catch you some specimen fish if you can contact them.

In clement weather, most coarse fish (but not bream) will rise in the water during the darker hours to take full advantage of the hatches of fly, as do trout and grayling. A nymph or dry fly fished carefully could produce the best results. For this reason, a floating line is usually more practical. But if you are fishing deep still water, a sinking line will help you to reach the bottom and fish more efficiently.

Most of the non-predatory fish shoal together in large numbers, and as a rule those you catch in a shoal will all be roughly the same size.

In rivers and streams, fish such as orfe, dace, chub, and several other species will rise to a dry fly and can provide very entertaining fishing.

Salt-Water Fish

Left: A bonefish taken on a crab-imitating lure. The change in colour of the sea in the background indicates where the ocean drops off and the flats begin. These are the feeding grounds of the bonefish at certain times of the day.

Below: Golden shrimp lures are very popular with most bonefish anglers. But there are many varieties of flies, and it is best to heed the advice of the local guides. Guides are an absolute necessity when fishing the flats for any type of fish.

To the avid flyfisher, the sea must represent the ultimate challenge, with its vast expanses of water and the mighty fish that dwell within them, whether they are fish sought for their size or for their fighting qualities.

As a rough and ready classification, we may divide the fish sought by fly into the exotic, which are out of reach of most everyday anglers, and the less exotic, which abound in all waters around the world. Like freshwater species, the salt-water kind have their game fish, but these do not belong to one family. They are fish renowned for their superior fighting ability and sometimes for their size. Such fish as the tunny, tarpon, permit, sailfish,

and some species of shark are regarded as game fish.

Sea Tackle

For flyfishing in the sea you will require tackle that has been proofed against corrosion at the manufactur-

Above: A bonefish cruises along as it searches the bottom for food.
Right: A fine catch of bonefish taken by an angler on fly.

ing stage. In contact with salt water, ordinary tackle would soon be destroyed or rendered useless. The usual types of fly rods may be used, although a strong one is necessary. Rings and reel fittings must be non-corrosive. Reels may be obtained already proofed. You should use a larger reel than usual in order to accommodate enough line for the greater depths fished and the longer runs that may be made by the fish.

At least some of the time you will need to use a line with either a lead core or a lead-impregnated coating. This will enable you to fish at a greater depth, and also go some way towards combating the stronger water

This typical bass fly displays the bright colours usually used to draw the attention of the fish away from all the natural food available. This hair wing also adds life, and the body is tapered to provide the bulk necessary to appeal to the fish as food.

currents. Both floating and sinking lines are used for sea flyfishing, depending on the fish and the type of water.

When there is a risk of contacting fish with strong jaws and teeth, the fly must be joined to the leader by a length of wire or heavy nylon known as a *trace*. The fly itself will be a large monstrosity in comparison with freshwater flies, designed only with the

magnificent fight on ordinary trout flyfishing gear. And in the estuaries you will find fish such as mullet and bass, and sometimes sea trout, which will take a well-fished fly and fight hard.

If you wish to extend your horizon and try something more formidable, there are always the sharks. Starting with the porbeagle, a member of the shark family, can be a thrilling

A contrast in flies used for sea fishing. The Johnson's Woolybugs (right) are rather plainer in appearance than the fly used for tempting bass (below). Sea flies are usually tied on straight-eyed, long-shanked nickel-plated hooks to prevent the corrosive influence of the salt water.

purpose of attracting the fish and arousing its feeding instincts. Most sea flies are white or incorporate a great deal of flash. Red and yellow are also popular colours.

Where and What

Around most of the world's coastlines you will find mackerel and often garfish, both of which will give a

introduction for the flyfisher, and then the blue shark, one of the smaller and more common types, which can be tempted in subtropical waters.

The more exotic fish, such as tarpon, bonefish, and permit, are popular quarries in the more tropical areas, such as the Caribbean, the Gulf of Mexico, and the Bahamas.

Fishing at Sea

It is usually more practical to flyfish in the open sea from a boat. And whatever the fish, local knowledge is essential for finding the fish and for safety.

With most species, fishing is a matter of trial and error in the same way as fishing deep water on a reservoir or lake. Just allow the line to sink to different depths until you make contact with fish. This applies whether you fish from the shore or from a boat.

If you decide to hunt shark on fly, it is advisable to use a large boat with an engine and to go with several companions. The boat is allowed to drift, and a strong trail of innards, blood, or minced oily fish is either thrown over the boat regularly ('chumming') or trailed in the water in a bag ('rubby-dubby'), or both. The

Left: A typical shark fly displaying the wire trace necessary to protect the leader from the fish's teeth. Above: A sand shark being played, but with plenty of fight still.

idea is that the shark are attracted by the scent, and smell up the trail to the boat, where they may be fished for. You could leave a fly to trail behind the boat, or you might prefer to wait until a shark is spotted and then cast to it. Either way, it can be a long wait—but worth it in the end if you are successful.

Stalking bonefish, tarpon, or permit is exciting but by no means easy, and requires skill and dedication. At some times of the day they frequent areas known as the flats. These are vast expanses of water, about knee-deep, next to the ocean drop-off. The water there is crystal clear, and the fish can be seen for some distance browsing over the bottom and picking up crabs or other edible items.

The problem is that these fish are extraordinarily shy and very wild. You must be very careful not to spook them by bad casting or careless wading. Most of this fishing is done in a flat-bottomed boat called a skiff, with a guide who is employed to find the fish for you. The skiff's engine is used to take it far out into the flats, and then it is poled like a punt until fish are spotted.

It is usually preferable to be in the water when the fish are in casting range, and it is often a good plan to have already cast the fly into what appears to be their path, to avoid causing any casting disturbance. Use a floating line on the flats, with a lot of backing. The flies, which do not need to be very much bigger than a

is possible.

It is as well to remember that this kind of fishing, with the patient stalking involved, has its disappointments. Sometimes, you will carefully stalk a school of fish, only to find that it either changes direction completely or is spooked by a faulty cast.

Other fish that provide sport for the flyfisher on the flats are shark and barracuda. These may also be stalked, or the barracuda may be found lying

Right: Two of the sea's most predatory and most sporting species. The fish on the left is a sand shark, and the other a barracuda. Both were taken in the Bahamas.

large freshwater lure, should be dressed approximately to represent sea creatures such as crabs or shrimps. Tarpon flies are tied with long, dyed hackles as 'wings', dressed the reverse way to normal, so that they open and close when retrieved and look like small fish.

When a fish reaches the fly, which may by then be resting on the bottom, move it with either a twitch or a long slow pull, depending on exactly how far away from it the fish is. The idea is that the fish will pick it up and move away. This is the time to strike. But hang on, because bonefish and permit particularly are renowned for their extraordinarily long and powerful runs. Hold the rod high to clear the line from the water as far as this

in wait for its prey. In any case, a large fly retrieved quickly will more than likely produce a response from these predators. Both grow to large proportions, and the barracuda is renowned for its speed and the way that it slams into the lure on the take.

Sport for All

Many other species of fish throughout the world are regularly sought after by anglers using flyfishing techniques. There are fish in the sea that will provide sport for every angler, without the need to travel to tropical or exotic regions. It is really just a matter of having sufficient dedication to exploit the available waters and to produce a technique that will catch the fish you want.

Advanced Angling

Once you have mastered the basic techniques of flyfishing, you may wish to progress further and seek larger fish. The best way to start 'specimen hunting', as it is called, is to fish a water where you know there are big fish present, and to concentrate on specific areas until you either achieve your objective or conclude that you might have better luck elsewhere. Success in flyfishing is really a matter of being in the right place at the right time with the right

Left: A fine limit bag of trout from Grafham Water, in England.
Below: By comparison, this beautifully marked brown trout from the River Torridge may seem small, but in difficult conditions, where presentation must be exact and the fight is hard, it is no less satisfying.

A marrow spoon being withdrawn.

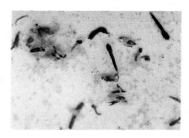

Stomach contents.

Spooning

The object of spooning a fish is to find out what it is feeding on. Then you can select your fly to imitate that food in an attempt to catch more fish.

The first step is to catch a fish for spooning. The marrow spoon is then inserted into the dead fish's mouth. You have to push it past the throat and as far as possible into the stomach, and then twist it and withdraw it. If the operation is successful, you will have part of the fish's stomach contents on the spoon. With a fish that has been feeding heavily, the items of food might be tightly packed together. In this case it is best to empty the contents first into water in a shallow, preferably white, receptacle, so that the food separates and examination is easier.

Sometimes spooning may not be necessary, because the mouth of the fish may be full of unswallowed food. At other times, the spoon might come up with just a kind of cloudy, jelly-like substance. This is an indication that the fish has not fed recently, and it is reasonable to continue to use the fly on which it was taken.

method and the right fly. At some time, with a lot of experience and perhaps not a little luck, you will satisfy all these factors and catch your big fish.

If you are fortunate enough to catch a record fish or a prize-winning specimen, make sure you get it weighed on a reliable and acceptable set of scales (not a spring-balance), with as many witnesses as you can muster (usually two will do). Once you have verification of the fish and its weight, you can submit a claim to the appropriate body for consideration.

You will probably enjoy having a photographic record of any fine specimen you catch, so it is a good idea to carry a camera with you on your expeditions. Always try to photograph the fish immediately after capture, when it will look its best. There are several ways of indicating the size of the fish, as you will see from the photographs in this book — by placing it next to some tackle, perhaps, or by having someone photograph you with it.

It is important to remember, though, that not all fish of merit have to be large. Taking a small trout under tricky conditions from a small stream often requires as much skill as landing a salmon several times the size in easier conditions.

Waiting for the signal to begin a national competition.

Competitions

Competition flyfishing brings out two qualities possessed by most anglers — the competitive spirit and camaraderie.

International flyfishing competitions have been held on a regular basis between England, Ireland, Scotland, and Wales since 1932, and a world wet-flyfishing competition is held annually on Lough Mask, in western Ireland. In addition to these events, it has now become fashionable, and is becoming more so, among clubs at local level to hold similar competitions, either amongst themselves or with other clubs.

The local flyfishing competitions are fished from either bank or boat. The international events are fished under strict rules from boat only, usually with a referee in each boat.

The object of the competitions is to catch the biggest weight of trout, and this may be accomplished with many small fish or perhaps with fewer larger ones. There are events for both individuals and teams.

Fishing is usually for a limited period, say from 10 a.m. to 6 p.m., and in boat competitions the only method allowed is casting the fly downwind on a short line from a sitting position. Four flies of a specified maximum size are allowed, and they may be wet or dry or a combination of both. It is more usual to fish three wet flies, although the bob-fly may be a bushy dry fly or heavily dressed wet fly in order to create an attracting wake.

This is, in effect, the traditional method of loch-style fishing. It would not be practicable to have a large number of boats all using different methods of flyfishing and with all kinds of flies. So to standardize the contests, the traditional style is employed.

The advantage of short-lining as in the traditional style is that your fly is cast a short distance down the wind to fish that are moving upwind towards you. You retrieve a short distance and then fish the cast out with your arm and the rod. For this reason, a long rod is an advantage, keeping all flies in the water or just dibbling the bob-fly through the surface. The line is then lifted off the water, and this should work the rod sufficiently to enable you to shoot the line immediately. As a result, false casting is minimized, and your fly spends more time in the water. This in turn means that it has more chance of being spotted by a fish.

There are other advantages of the short line. Because there is more chance of producing a fly in front of a fish, it is more likely to take it. With a long cast, the line would probably land above the fish and scare it. And because both anglers remain seated, presenting a lower profile, the fish tend to come close to the boat. Another advantage is that, because there is less false casting, there is not as much rod and line movement to scare the fish. Stealth is the secret of this type of fishing.

Bank-fishing contests are more relaxed in their rules, because policing them would be difficult. Most competitions simply stipulate a time to start and a time to weigh in. The objectives are the same as for boat-fishing.

Above: An official weighs the catch of an entrant in a flyfishing competition. The winner is the one who has caught the greatest weight of trout, irrespective of how many fish make up the catch. Competitors have a set time in which to fish, and there are usually rules specifying the number and type of flies that may be fished. National championships are held in several countries, and there are also international events.

Right: A proud competitor with his winning catch.

What to Wear and Take

Before setting out on a fishing trip, it is worth spending a little time planning what to wear and what to take in addition to the main fishing tackle (rods, lines, flies, etc.).

Flyfishing can become extremely tiring towards the end of a long day, and to be comfortable in as many ways as possible at that time is a great help. Waders, for example, are often essential, but they can be cumbersome, so do not take them if they are not needed. You will find it much more comfortable to wear the lightest footwear possible, and it will increase the enjoyment of your fishing. The same applies to all clothing. In cold or wet weather, wear clothing that will keep you dry and warm but will not impede you.

A multipocketed waistcoat can be a great aid to efficiency as well as to comfort. Not only will it save you from carrying an unwieldy tackle bag, but it will ensure that the essential items are close at hand when you need them in a hurry.

The prevailing weather will, of course, determine your choice of clothing to a certain extent. Some form of headgear to protect you from rain or blazing sun is recommended. And another good friend of the angler is a plain towel. This has many uses apart from drying yourself with, such as wrapping it round your neck to keep out the rain.

Anything that helps your concentration is an asset, and this applies to food and drink. Always take enough to last you for the time you will be fishing.

You will need a tackle bag large enough to hold your tackle, with a comfortable shoulder strap for carrying it. You should also take a bag for the fish you hope to catch. The ideal bag is one that can be wetted to keep the fish as fresh as possible, but avoid polythene bags.

Finally, there are the bits and pieces of tackle that, though important, are not all essential every time you go fishing. You should always carry a priest in order to dispatch a fish immediately on capture and thus minimize any suffering it might experience out of the water. Forceps are useful for extracting difficult or deeply set hooks. Scissors, of course, have many uses, such as cutting line. (Always trim waste line to tiny lengths before throwing it away, or take it home, because it can injure wildlife.) Other useful items include line grease for floating-line work, a compound to make the leader sink, dry-fly floatant, and spare tackle such as leaders and reels.

Opposite: An angler about to start a day's fishing on open water should be well protected against all possible weather conditions. All accessories, including food and drink, are being carried on this occasion, and there is still a large amount of gear in the car. A wise precaution in case of heavy rain is a change of clothing.

Glossary

Action (rod) The way in which a rod behaves when casting; for example, a *tip-action* rod concentrates most flexibility in the tip.

AFTM scale The standard for rating the weight of fly-lines and for matching line to rod.

Alevin The young of the trout and, particularly, the salmon.

Attractor A fly that does not imitate any form of life but arouses a fish's aggression.

Hooked on an attractor fly

Backing line A long length of line connecting the fly-line to the reel; for use when a fish makes a long run.

Baggot Term used for a salmon that has returned to the river and remains there for some time; a rogue fish.

Bird's-nest A tangle of line.

Bob-fly The top dropper.

Bubble float A device used usually in conjunction with monofilament line to provide weight to cast a fly with coarse tackle. It may be filled with water.

Bulge The displacement of the surface of the water by a fish with its back when feeding just subsurface; fish feeding in this way are said to be *humping*.

Centrepin reel A reel that revolves round a central axis.

Chalk stream A stream or river that is clear because it rises in chalk hills, from springs, and is seldom affected in level to much extent by rainfall.

Check A ratchet or drag that may be used to increase or relax the tension on a reel to provide resistance to a running fish.

Coarse fish Any fish that lives in freshwater and is not a member of the salmon family.

Cover a fish To cast a fly so that the fish will see it.

Dapping The method of allowing the fly to blow in front of you and just skid along the surface as the line is taken by the wind.

Double-hauling A casting technique where the free hand accelerates the line during the cast to provide more distance.

Double taper A fly-line that tapers from the middle to a thinner point at each end so that it is reversible.

Drag Situation that occurs when a dry fly skids across the surface instead of floating with the current.

Drift fishing Fishing from a boat allowed to drift with the wind.

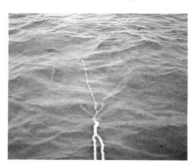

Drogue

Drogue An underwater parachute-type of device attached to a boat to slow the drift or hold it in a certain position as it drifts.

Dropper An additional fly on the leader.

Dry fly An artificial fly that floats on the water surface.

Body of fly formed by dubbing

Dubbing In fly-tying, the twisting of a furry material round the thread to form a body.

Dun An ephemerid fly before it becomes a *spinner*.

Ephemerid One of a group of real water-bred, upwing flies that are short-lived, such as the mayfly.

False-casting The process of lengthening the line in the air until enough is 'aerialized' to make the final cast.

Fast-recovery reel A reel geared to revolve the drum in a higher ratio per turn of the handle; also called *multiplier reel*.

Figure-eighting A method of bunching the line in the palm of the hand when retrieving; an excellent way to maintain constant movement of the fly.

Finnock Local name for sea trout.

Flash The reflecting of light by a fly due to the inclusion of tinsel in the dressing

Floatant A substance applied to dry flies to ensure their long-floating qualities; also used to make lines and leaders float.

Applying floatant

Floater or **floating fly** Other terms for a dry fly.

Fly-line The weighted line used in fly-fishing.

Forward taper See *Weight-forward taper*.

Foul-hooked Of a fish, hooked anywhere but in the mouth.

Fry The early stages of any fish.

Gaff An instrument, consisting of a metal hook attached to a stout pole, used for landing heavy fish.

Game fish Of freshwater fish, a term used for members of the salmon family; in salt water, generally any fish of fine sporting ability.

Ghillie (or **gillie**) A non-fishing companion, usually a local who is there to offer advice and help, provided by the owner of a water.

Grass To land a salmon.

Greased line A method used in low-water conditions to fish for salmon. The term was used of silk lines which were greased to make them float.

Grilse Term for a salmon making its first return from the sea, after 12–18 months there, to spawn.

Hackle A single feather from a hen or cock, or the feather tied on a fly immediately behind the eye of the hook.

Hand-tailing Method of landing a salmon, after playing it into shallow water, by seizing it by the wrist of the tail.

Hatch A large quantity of the same flies all coming off the water; also, a series of boards placed across a stream to regulate the flow.

Humping See *Bulge*.

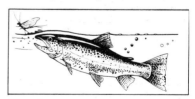

Humping

Imago The final stage of an insect. See also *Spinner*.

Imitator A fly that represents a form of food that a fish may be feeding on.

Kelt Term for a salmon after spawning; usually an ugly-looking fish, which if caught should always be returned alive.

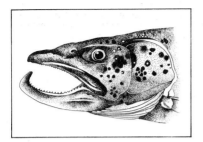

A fish with kype

Kype The hooked lower jaw of a male salmon or trout acquired with old age.
Landing net A net on a pole in which the played-out fish is brought ashore.
Larva The underwater stage of some forms of insect.
Lateral line The line along a fish's flank through which it senses vibrations and movement in the water.
Leader The length of line connecting the fly-line to the fly.
Lie The resting place of a fish, or what it may consider to be its territory.
Limit The maximum number or weight of fish the rules of the water permit to be killed.
Lure A large wet fly designed to tempt predatory fish, either as an attractor or by representing fry.
Marrow spoon A device used to extract the stomach contents of fish to see what they are feeding on, so that the food may be imitated.
Mending line Throwing more line upstream after the final cast has landed, to create slack and obviate drag.
Milt The fluid exuded by a male fish to fertilize the female's eggs.
Minnow A small fish found almost everywhere in freshwater, and an important dietary item of most fish.
Monofilament Ordinary single-strand nylon fishing line.
Multiplier reel See *Fast-recovery reel.*
Nymph Angler's term for the stage in the life-cycle of some water-bred insects, after the egg and before the winged stage; imitation fly of this stage.
Parachute fly A dry fly with its hackle tied parallel with the water's surface.
Parr Term for the early stage of a salmon, when it lives in freshwater before making its first journey to the sea.

Playing a fish 'Fighting' the fish after hooking it so that it may be landed.
Point The slim tip of a leader; see also *Tippet.*
Point fly The fly fished at the farthest point of the leader on a team; also known as the *tail fly.*
Priest A weighted club used to kill a landed fish with a blow to the back of the head.
Pupa The final stage of some insects, such as sedges and midges, before the winged stage.
Put down a fish To cause a fish to stop feeding, usually by fishing clumsily and scaring it into inactivity or into bolting.
Redd A nest in which the eggs are laid, made in the gravel of a stream bed by the twisting motions of a salmon or trout.
Resting a fish Leaving a fish after it has been 'put down' in the hope that it will begin feeding again later.
Retrieving Fishing the fly back towards you by recovering the line.
Rings The guides whipped to a rod to enforce the rod's action and through which the line passes.
Rise The action of a fish coming up to take a fly from the water's surface; collectively, a period when fish are feeding avidly on the surface.
Scissors The intersection of the upper and lower jaws of a fish, the best place to hook it.
Shooting-taper or **shooting-head** Flyline with sufficient length to work the rod, attached to a length of lighter line as backing, usually less than half the length of a full fly-line; used for casting long distances.

Parachute fly

Sink-tip A floating fly-line with the forward part—usually about 10ft (3m) —treated to sink; for fishing just sub-surface.

Smolt A young salmon ready to migrate to the sea for the first time.

Smutting The taking of minute insects in the surface film by a fish.

Snake cast A deliberately erratic cast designed to avoid *drag*; made by waving the rod tip from side to side as the line is released on the final cast.

Spate A flood or an increase in the water flowing in a river.

Spawning The laying of eggs by a female fish and the fertilizing of them by the male.

Specimen fish A fish that is of exceptional weight for a particular water and in good condition.

Spey cast The longest cast that can be made without the line extending behind the rod (from the River Spey, in Scotland).

Spinner (fly) The final stage, after the winged dun, in the life-cycle of upwing flies; known, after mating, as 'spent spinners'.

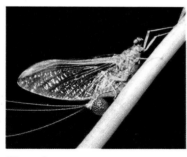

Olive spinner

'Spook' a fish To frighten a fish into bolting from the area.

Streamer fly A lure that has long wings extending behind the hook bend; usually made of hackle feathers.

Strike Set the hook into a fish that has taken the fly.

Stringer A clip, attached to string, inserted through the lower jaw of a fish and used to carry it when dead or to peg it in the water to retain it.

Sub-imago A fly of the upwing type in the dun phase, prior to becoming a spinner.

'Sulking' Term used of a hooked fish that takes to the bottom or hides behind a snag and refuses to budge.

Sunken fly See *Wet fly*.

Tail fly See *Point fly*.

Tailer Instrument used to secure a salmon by the wrist of its tail in order to land it.

Take The taking of the fly by a fish.

Tandem hooks

Tandem hook Two (or more) hooks tied in tandem behind each other to provide additional hooking capacity.

Taper A tapered fly-line or leader.

Team of flies A number of flies, usually three or four, fished on the same leader.

Tippet The thin end of the leader, often knotted into it; also called the *point*.

Torpedo-head line See *Weight-forward taper*.

Trace A length of wire or heavier line used to protect the leader from the teeth of predators.

Treble hook A hook that has three bends and barbs brazed together to give all-round hooking capacity.

Trolling Trailing the line behind a moving boat.

Trophy fish A *specimen fish*.

Tube fly A fly dressed on a tube through which the line is threaded and then tied to a treble hook.

Wading Entering the water to gain distance or to overcome bankside obstacles.

Wake fly A dry fly that is pulled over or through the surface to create a wake.

Weight-forward taper A line that has its weight concentrated in the forward section, used for casting longer distances; also called *forward taper* or *torpedo-head line*.

Wet fly An artificial fly fished beneath the surface; also called a *sunken fly*.

Window The extent of a fish's vision.

Index

ACKNOWLEDGEMENTS

The author and publishers wish to thank the following for their kind help in supplying photographs:

Bruce Coleman 77. Bob Church 11 centre right, bottom, 71 bottom, 102 bottom, 107, 108, 109 top, 110 centre, 112–113, 114 top. Colorspot 40 top right. Government of British Columbia 95. G. L. Carlisle 59, 74 bottom, 77 top, 78 bottom left and right, 88 top, 93, 101 bottom, 106. Nick Cranfield 11, 49, 53 top, bottom right, 63, 66, 72, 74 top, 94, 96, 98, 102 top, 103, 104 top, 115 top right. Bernard Cecil Hall 52, 76 top, 79 top. Trevor Housby 75, 83, 120 left. Frank Iredale 46, 115 top left. Mike Millman 26, 84, 109 bottom, 110 top, 111 top, 112. Neil Nevison 73 top, 80, 89, 108 top left, 110 bottom. Arthur Oglesby 8, 10, 12 top left and right, 16, 20 bottom, 32 bottom, 41, 53 bottom left, 69, 86 bottom, 88 bottom, 90, 91, 97, 100, 104 bottom. Taff Price 65, 78 top, 87, 111 bottom. Roy Shaw 58, 71 top, 123 left. Peter Stone 17, 50, 51, 53 centre left, 76 bottom, 85. Natural Science Photos 27, 30, 56, 64, 81 top, 121 bottom.

Cover: G. L. Carlisle

All other photographs supplied by the author and Rosa Furzer.

Artwork by Colin Newman (Linden Artists).

Picture Research: Tracy Rawlings.